Witchcraft in Massachusetts

Reasons for Concluding That the Act of 1711, Reversing the Attainders of the Persons Convicted of Witchcraft in Massachusetts in the Year 1692, Became a Law

Being a Reply to Supplementary Notes, Etc., by George H. Moore, LL.D.

Reprinted from the Proceedings of the Massachusetts Historical Society

Abner Cheney Goodell, Jr.

HERITAGE BOOKS
2020

HERITAGE BOOKS
AN IMPRINT OF HERITAGE BOOKS, INC.

Books, CDs, and more—Worldwide

For our listing of thousands of titles see our website
at
www.HeritageBooks.com

A Facsimile Reprint
Published 2020 by
HERITAGE BOOKS, INC.
Publishing Division
5810 Ruatan Street
Berwyn Heights, Md. 20740

Copyright © 1997 Heritage Books, Inc.

Originally published:
Cambridge
John Wilson and Son
University Press
1884

— Publisher's Notice —
In reprints such as this, it is often not possible to remove blemishes from the original. We feel the contents of this book warrant its reissue despite these blemishes and hope you will agree and read it with pleasure.

International Standard Book Number
Paperbound: 978-0-7884-0816-8

WITCHCRAFT IN MASSACHUSETTS.

At a meeting of the MASSACHUSETTS HISTORICAL SOCIETY, held March 13, 1884, in reply to a communication presented by Dr. GEORGE H. MOORE, of New York, Mr. A. C. GOODELL, Jr., made the following remarks:—

As might have been expected, our learned and ingenious associate has given us all that can be shown or surmised in support of his original proposition, that the act of 1711 never became a law; and yet it seems to me that, fairly weighed against what has been shown on the other side, his arguments do not preponderate.

Admiration of the skill with which he hurled some of his shafts, to say nothing of a sense of peril, quite distracted my attention from some other of his points, made with equal felicity of expression. In short, I feel overborne by the torrent of eloquence to which we have listened, and am conscious of inability to rally, for the moment, so as to do justice to him or myself.

But let us glance at the issue as it stands. To remove a doubt never entertained until Dr. Moore denied the existence of the act in question, but which, starting from such a source, merits the most careful consideration, I have shown, first, from the journals of the Governor and Council, commonly called the "General Court Records," an entry of the passage of the bill in question, to be enacted; second, I have referred to a contemporaneous copy, in the handwriting of the Secretary of the Province, filed in the office of the Clerk of the Courts, at Salem, where it has remained since 1711; third, I have called attention to three contemporaneous references to this act, by different parties interested;[1] and, fourth, I have produced, as the final test, a copy of the act, printed on a single leaf in the year 1713, — which copy, it is admitted, bears on its face conclusive evidence of having been impressed from the types of Bartholomew Green, then printer to the Governor and Council.

Now, to invalidate the last of these concurrent evidences, which taken together impress me as decisive, my friend, here, asks you to believe that the act, of which we have a heliotype in our Proceedings, was surreptitiously printed. He does not suggest the motive, nor indicate with certainty the possible author of this deed. Perhaps he would have us believe that it was done by the printer's devil, to mark the end of an invidious rivalry with the recently dethroned Prince of Darkness, and to celebrate the absoluteness of his own less vindictive, though not always less provoking sway. However, I do not intend to carry my criticism beyond the sure support of incontrovertible facts. I am even willing to admit that I cannot conceive how the critical reasons for questioning the authenticity of the printed copy could be more ably or thoroughly presented than they have been in the paper just read; and yet I feel confident they do not in your minds overcome the strong presumption arising from the mutually corroborating circumstances which attest the genuineness of this copy, and from the absence of any conceivable motive for perpetrating the highhanded forgery which the alleged clandestine operations with Bartholomew Green's types would imply.

I will not then attempt to follow the critical argument in detail, but content myself with calling your attention to a fact which, if clearly borne in mind, may serve to lessen the rigor

---

[1] Dr. Moore infers (Proc. Mass. Hist. Soc., vol. xxi. p. 88), that, because in two of these instances the petitioners pray that certain names may be "inserted in the act," the act had not been actually passed. But this is hardly a necessary inference, since the act and an act in addition thereto would, by legal construction, constitute but one act; and therefore it is not difficult to conceive that the "advisers" of the petitioners may have seen no impropriety in suggesting such "modification of, or addition to, a statute which was already a law of the land." Again, both of the petitioners describe the act either as "the late act," or "the act lately made;" and one of them expressly prays that application may be made, "*at the next session*" of the General Court, to have her name inserted. Now what is the purpose of an act *in addition*, etc., but to make "modifications of, or additions to," some statute already enacted? And is there any rule limiting the operation of such an act so as to exclude the insertion of additional names?

of the rules by which the argument should be conducted. It is not pretended that the printed act was one of a series of acts published by *authority;* but, on the contrary, it is assumed to have been printed, a year or two after its passage, probably to meet the demands of persons interested, who could not be so conveniently and cheaply supplied with manuscript copies.

Although bills of attainder after the Revolution of 1688 were considered public acts,—notwithstanding they had ceased to be of the nature of conclusive judgments, as formerly, but were in terms conditional and in their operation dependent upon some future act of the accused or some prospective judicial proceeding against him, — bills to reverse or set aside attainders were classed with private acts, both in Old and New England.[1]

Nothing, therefore, against the existence of such an act should be inferred from the fact that it does not appear in the first volume of the new edition of the Province Laws, since, according to the arrangement announced by the editors in their preface,[2] it properly belongs in the appendix, with other private acts, including the similar act of 1703. The title of this act does not, indeed, appear in the list of titles of private acts in that volume, and for the reasons I have heretofore given;[3] but upon Mr. Sainsbury's discovery of printed copies of the missing public acts of the same year, respecting which, in the matter of the Governor's assent, the record was similarly defective, it was immediately put in the list of titles of private acts reserved for the appendix, although it was too late to make the proper change in the printed volume. This was done in the hope that before the appendix should be printed, the certainty of the act's having been passed would be established; which happened, to the satisfaction of the editors, when the printed copy in question, exactly corresponding with the manuscript copy at Salem, came to their knowledge.

The fact that it was a private act should also cause us to treat with distrust any arguments against its genuineness founded upon discrepancies, in formal and typographical

---

[1] This was the case with the bills annulling the attainders of Lord Russell, Algernon Sidney, and Lady Alice Lisle (1 W. & M., 1st sess.); and with the provincial act, referred to by Dr. Moore, reversing the attainder of Abigail Faulkner and others, passed in 1703.

[2] Page xxviii.   [3] Proc. Mass. Hist. Soc., vol. xx. p. 290.

details, between this copy and the public acts printed in the regular series. There being no absolute or customary standard for private as well as for public acts, all those departures from uniformity which have been disclosed by the expert scrutiny of Dr. Moore are not shown to be less compatible with honesty on the part of the person or persons who printed or procured the printing of this copy, than is the absence of page-numbers, or than would be the presence of any peculiarity in the signature, paper, or press-work.

The same circumstance, moreover, weakens the force of another objection which Dr. Moore appears to think, if not insuperable, at least formidable; and that is, that the act in question does not appear to have been laid before the ministers of the crown. Private acts, not being regularly printed, often failed, possibly sometimes on that account, to reach the Privy Council. This is evident from the demands occasionally made for exemplifications of such acts, upon the Governor or the Secretary of the Province, by the Lords of Trade or from the Council Board. Hence less importance should be attached to the failure to discover the mention of any particular private act in the Public Record Office. Besides, to insist on the importance of such a defect is to apply a rule which will equally unsettle the authenticity of several public acts. For instance, since no list of the acts of 1711 has been found in the British archives,—if, indeed, any such list was actually transmitted,—the proof of the passage of three of the public acts of that year must rest upon the existence of a printed copy or copies; for this, meagre as it may seem, is all the evidence that we have of the fact that these acts really passed the Province seal. Now, if this evidence is inadmissible, the acts must fall; there being no record showing that the Governor assented to them, and neither the original bill nor the engrossment of either having been preserved.

Yet Dr. Moore says these "are known to have been printed contemporaneously, in due course, and by regular official authority." He fails, however, to add that this knowledge is derived from precisely the same kind of evidence upon which I claim to found my knowledge of the passage of the act to reverse the attainders. And while he informs us that two of these acts are in the supplements of the edition of 1699, he modestly refrains from telling us that only one perfect collection of these supplements exists, which he, its fortunate possessor, esteems an adequate reward for the expense of time and money, and for the great learning and ingenuity with which for many years his bibliographical researches for its completion were conducted.

Surely our friend's comparison of the "status" of the act for reversing the attainders with that of other acts — for instance, the act for enforcing the order of June 12, 1711 — should have been extended beyond the bare declaration, in five words, with which he disposes of the former. The category of each is identical; and if one is to be summarily "relegated to the limbo of imperfect legislation," he should show with all possible cogency of reasoning and fulness of illustration sufficient grounds for exempting the public act from the same fate. The difficulty of the task should rather have induced than excused the attempt; for we cannot be presumed to know what circumstance in favor of the public act overbalances, in his mind, the cumulative evidence afforded by the presence, legitimately, in a public office, of a contemporaneous copy of the private act in the handwriting of the Secretary of the Province and by him indorsed "Copy," and minuted "examined," while not a scrap is referred to indicating that the public act was ever officially recognized.

I shall say something more on this head presently, after I have considered the objections which Dr. Moore discovers on the face of the printed act.

I am content to allow his criticisms upon the "style and method and literary treatment" of the act to pass for what they are worth, with the single observation, which I think he will approve, that of all literature in the world statute-books of the early part of the last century are the least likely to afford specimens of elegant diction, and that the frequent occurrence of acts to amend and explain those early statutes sufficiently attests the crudeness of the efforts of the average law-maker of that day, both in Old or New England, to frame his bills so as to express his intentions with ordinary certainty.

Therefore, after remarking, in order to show its slight significance, that the omission of the Christian name of Goodwife Corey was a piece of carelessness which, though unusual, can be capped by grosser instances even in the public acts of a much later day,[1] I proceed to examine the more important internal evidence which Dr. Moore points out as tending to prove the spuriousness of the act.

And, first, of the improbability of the passage of this act by the General Court, because the subject-matter belonged exclusively to the cognizance of Parliament. If Dr. Moore's views respecting the exclusive authority of Parliament to pass bills reversing attainders were well grounded — which I do not admit — he himself furnishes me with a conclusive answer in the present case, where he says: "Of course the fact that the General Court of Massachusetts had no right to pass such an act is no evidence that they refrained from the attempt," — an opinion admirably sustained by their passing, eight years before, the act to reverse the attainders of Abigail Faulkner and others, which our friend has printed, at length, in the appendix to his Notes on the History of Witchcraft, etc. It is therefore unnecessary to discuss the constitutionality of the act, which, by the way, was not questioned by the Solicitor-General of England when the act of 1703 was laid before him by command of the Lords of Trade, — a proceeding which Dr. Moore too hastily assumes could not have happened.

Nor need we inquire what differences in the organic law of the respective provinces of New York and Massachusetts Bay, or in the political ideas which prevailed in those provinces, or what dissimilarity in the special circumstances of any given case, may at any time have induced the legislatures of the two provinces to differ in their action. But it may be observed that in both provinces at that time the supremacy of Parliament was generally recognized. Its power, if not its right, to meddle, temporarily at least, with the internal affairs of either province, and even to disregard the qualified autonomy granted by the charter of Massachusetts, was not denied except by a very small party, constituting, however, the germ which slowly expanded into that resistless band of patriots which succeeded to power and glory in the Revolution. Nor should I omit to say that Dudley's change of opinion between the time of his signing the act of 1703 and the culmination of the movement for redressing the grievances of 1692 is not to be taken for granted.

[1] For instance, Prov. Laws, 1757-58, chap. 15; 1760-61, chap. 7; and 1768, chap. 16, § 1.

Dr. Moore discovers another badge of spuriousness in the declaration, in the preamble of the act, that the survivors were "lying still under the like Sentence of the said Court and liable to have the same Executed upon them," which, he says, is false, inasmuch as the survivors had all been pardoned. Of course he does not mean to have us understand that the preamble expressly puts *all* the survivors in this category by the word "others," which, as the context shows, may have been intended to embrace only a few of the persons convicted and sentenced, — that is, "attainted."

But how many pardons were actually granted? and where is the record evidence? When were the charters of pardon pleaded? or in what manner were they communicated after sentence? Has my friend any other evidence that pardons were granted than the declarations of Mather and Calef, and the representations of some of the petitioners for redress? If he has, he ought to have adduced it to support his charge of falsehood. If he has not, we are bound to challenge the correctness of the inference he would force upon us, that all the survivors were pardoned.

Of the witnesses I have referred to, Calef alone implies that all the surviving convicts were pardoned; but the unsupported testimony of all of them would be entirely insufficient to prove that Governor Phips violated his instructions, and set an example which was never followed by his successors.

The pardon of felonies was a prerogative of the crown, which could only be delegated by express language; and if pardons were granted by the Governor without such authority, the act was *ultra vires*. The authority has not been shown here; nor is it to be presumed, for, although the provincial governors were usually authorized to grant pardons in all cases except treason and wilful murder, the authority could not be lawfully exercised in this province without special permission, in any case where the effect of the pardon would be to remit a forfeiture of more than £10 in value.[1] Hutchinson, who understood the law relating to this branch of the prerogative, does not pretend that Phips pardoned any of the condemned. His words are: "Those the governor reprieved,

---

[1] See Proc. Mass. Hist. Soc., vol. xx. p. 148, and note.

for the King's mercy."[1] Undoubtedly, as Hutchinson says, the three persons[2] convicted at the January term of the Superior Court of Judicature at Salem were reprieved; and some of the accused perhaps were pardoned, after a reprieve, by royal charter or mandate, as appears to have been the case with Abigail Faulkner, who had been attainted by the Court of Oyer and Terminer. But what evidence is there that all the other attainted persons were pardoned? And if they were not pardoned, the statement in the preamble remains unshaken by this attempt to impeach it.[3]

But Dr. Moore goes further, and declares that neither the printed act nor the manuscript copy at Salem "has any provision or provisions 'in favour of' the sufferers or their representatives, 'respecting their Estates.'"

I hardly know how to account for this assertion; it is so directly at variance with what I had supposed every lawyer would frankly admit was the inseparable incident of attainders everywhere throughout the realm and the dominions of England. Would our friend have us believe that no forfeiture and no escheat followed the attainders of 1692? If so, here again I am compelled to confess my ignorance of his authority, and to express my regret that he has passed over the subject so lightly in his paper.

We must not lose sight of the fact that all who suffered the extreme penalty of the law in 1692 were condemned before the passage of the act "setting forth general privileges," by which escheats and forfeitures in cases of felony were abolished, and that this act was subsequently disallowed by the Privy Council because of this very clause which was declared

---

[1] Vol. ii. p. 61.

[2] Dr. Moore's quotation from Hutchinson respecting the characters of these persons is liable, as separated by him from the context, to be misunderstood. The historian is not comparing them with the whole world, but with their companions. If they were thus, relatively, "the worst characters," they may still have been very decent people, as, in point of fact, I believe they were. See Proc. Mass. Hist. Soc., vol. xxi. p. 88, n. 3.

[3] The "pardon" which Calef refers to, and the "discharge" mentioned by others, were probably one and the same thing. Hutchinson gives us an idea of the blind deference paid to persons in authority, in the romantic incident which he relates of the release of a prisoner by the Governor's lady, who forged a warrant to accomplish her purpose with the prison-keeper. The story, which seems to be true, justifies the inference that the Governor was supposed to have unlimited authority in the matter of discharging prisoners. Hence, too, the peculiarity of the final jail-delivery on which Hutchinson briefly comments.

by them to be "repugnant to the laws of England."[1] That act was not made retroactive expressly or by necessary implication.

Now, whatever may have been the practice in this Province after the passage of this act, and however convincing now appear to us the reasons that may be offered to show that a similar provision in the colonial "Body of Liberties" was operative under the new charter, it is certain that neither in Massachusetts nor at Whitehall did the notion at that time prevail that the "lands and heritages" of the condemned were exempt from forfeiture and escheat. Moreover, the act clearly contains nothing to prevent the " corruption of blood."

For my own part, I know of no reason for doubting that the attainders following the judgments pronounced against the persons convicted of witchcraft by the Court of Oyer and Terminer not only involved the forfeiture of all lands and other corporeal hereditaments, "for a year and a day, and waste," but that the real estate of the condemned escheated to the king, who, by the tenure of "free and common socage," as of the royal "Manor of East Greenwich," under which all lands in Massachusetts were held, was the immediate lord. This escheat, moreover, though not strictly a forfeiture, was an absolute sequestration of the realty; and, notwithstanding no actual entry may have been made, upon information or otherwise, and no record of "office found"[2] remains, the estates of those who were attainted were, according to the maxim *Nullum tempus occurrit regi*, forever liable to seizure unless a pardon specially restoring the escheated lands should be granted by the crown, or unless the attainder should be removed by an act of the legislature.

Until the enactment of a proper bill of reversal and restitution, however, the blood of the condemned remained "corrupted," so that neither could he be the vehicle for the transmission of property by descent, nor his posterity take from him by inheritance. A pardon, whatever effect it might have had when granted with apt words and a special design

---

[1] See note to 1692-93, chap. 11 in vol. i. of Province Laws; also Proc. Mass. Hist. Soc., vol. xx. p. 282, note †.

[2] "Where one is actually attainted, and his blood corrupted, and dies seized in fee, his lands cannot descend, but vest in the king without office found." Dane's Abr.; and see 4 Coke's Rep. [58 a].

to waive the escheat, could never avail to restore the forfeiture, or purge the blood of its " corruption."

Citations might be multiplied almost infinitely to show the utter insufficiency of a pardon from the king himself to avoid the consequences of attainder. In the language of Blackstone, which Dr. Moore has quoted, "Nothing can restore or purify the blood when once corrupted," even if a pardon be allowed "after attainder, but the high and transcendent power of Parliament."[1] In this Province, of course, the General Court performed this parliamentary function.

Nor did attainders operate solely to the injury of the condemned and his kindred; for as they invariably had relation " to the time of the fact committed," they avoided all subsequent conveyances and incumbrances of real estate by the condemned; and as some of the diabolical practices alleged in the indictments in 1692 dated back many years, the attainders may have subverted the intervening titles of creditors and innocent purchasers.

That these direful effects were understood and dreaded at that time is shown by the horrible nature of Giles Corey's punishment, who, to avoid the lasting and ruinous consequences of attainder, bravely accepted the awful alternative of the *peine forte et dure*.

If, then, I am right in my opinion that the act in question was necessary (and it is not material whether this necessity really existed or not, if the legislature believed it did) to secure immunity from this terrible ban, the " quietus," as Dr. Moore calls it, which the last paragraph of the act contains (the protection of the executive officers concerned in the prosecutions of the alleged witches), is by no means "the most important provision of the whole act." Nor is that exemption from lawsuits, even, to be condemned as inequitable, if the purposes of the act in other respects were fully carried out, since the grant of full compensation to the sufferers would unquestionably be good ground for denying them any further remedy.

I dismiss the topic of the declaration in the preamble with a brief recapitulation, to show more explicitly the complete antagonism between Dr. Moore's views and mine on this head.

---

[1] Commentaries, bk. iv. chap. xxxi. § 4. See also *ibid.*, chap. xxvi. p. 337, and chap. xxix. p. 376.

While he detects in this declaration a falsehood and a badge of fraud, to me it offers strong internal evidence of genuineness, because the truth it expresses imparts to the act a *raison d'être* and the color of necessity. He thinks that the " report" was the only legislative proceeding " in favour of " the " Estates" of the sufferers, while to me the report and the vote accepting it seem intended only to repair damage to the person and to chattels, and leave the " Estates " to be restored by the operation of a formal act, such as the one before us.

While in this train of thought, and before proceeding to the consideration of details less relevant, I turn to a paragraph of Dr. Moore's which I wish could not be construed even into the semblance of unkindness. I cannot think my frank and genial friend would for a moment intentionally indulge in unwarrantably severe reflections upon the character or conduct of the dead, to whom, in the performance of the sacred duty of critic or historiographer, he must perforce assign a place in his *tableaux* of the past. I am therefore willing to believe that it is my own perversity that detects a shade of injustice in his expressed opinion of the main purpose of " the wretched remnants "— of the families which were broken and scattered by the witch persecutions — in applying to the General Court. Yet, nevertheless, his words affect me painfully. He surely is conscious of the fealty he owes, as a man and a scholar, to that imperative law which forbids the ascription of unworthy motives without clear and convincing evidence. Am I wrong when I believe that the touching words of those petitioners were sincere, and that the declaration of the children of Rebecca Nurse, that " the principal thing wherein we desire restitution " is " the removing . . . the reproach " which the name of their dear mother " and the name of her posterity lyes under," only echoed the general sentiment of the petitioners ? If I err herein, it is because I do not repudiate the charitable rule, and discredit their own professions. But where would be my warrant for repudiating that rule ?

Why must I read between the lines something that shall falsify the professions of Francis Faulkner and nineteen others, who join in a petition to the General Court " that something may be publickly done to take off infamy from the names and memory of those who have suffered, . . . that none of their surviving relations, nor their posterity, may suffer reproach upon that account"? Why should I question the sincerity of the declaration of the Corey family that "that which is grieuous to us is that we are not only impoverished but also reproached, *and so may be to all generations, and that wrongfully . . . unless something be done for the removal thereof*," — or of the prayer of Isaac Estey and twenty-one others, that an act be passed to "*restore the reputations to the posterity of the sufferers*"?

When, in 1710, Estey said "this world can never make me any compensation," for the loss of his wife; and the poor man, Ephraim Wildes, declared that though his loss was £20 he was willing to take £14, "*considering our names may be repaired;*" and William Hobbs offered to reduce his claim from £40 to £10, for a like consideration; and Mary Bradbury's sons ask that the name of their good mother may be inserted in "*the bill for taking off the attainder;*"[1] and Charles Burroughs, Philip English, John Tarbell, Abraham Foster, Elizabeth Johnson, Thomas Carrier, Samuel Wardwell, and John and Joseph Parker make the same request; and the Rev. Thomas Barnard and eleven other ministers join in proposing to the General Court to consider whether something may not and ought not to be publicly done " to clear the good name and reputation " of some of the sufferers, — was *money* all they were after? Was Rebekah Fowle *feigning* when she urged that the business of compensation be quickly disposed of, because " every discourse on this melancholy subject doth but give a fresh wound to my bleeding heart"? I thank God that my respect for human nature, and my regard for what I consider the true historical method, alike forbid that I should believe it!

The traditions preserved by the posterity of these good

---

[1] As for the compensation, what can be more unselfish than the request of the Bradburys to the committee ? — " We doubt not but some others might suffer more in their estates ; and it seems very just and reasonable that restitution be, in some measure, made as far as the case will bear; and, therefore, we would not discourage so just and good a design by any excessive demands, *but rather comply with anything which your Honers shall think meet to allow*," etc. This was the general feeling, though there was some contention in the Burroughs family about the right of the widow to the lion's share, she having transferred all Burroughs's effects to another husband.

people and by the descendants of their neighbors corroborate the testimony of their faded, perhaps tear-stained, petitions still in the public files. Even in the pages of contemporary history, their pecuniary losses make an inconspicuous figure in the list of wrongs. The sums finally awarded to them seem miserably small and inadequate; but there is evidence directly tending to show that even this pittance they themselves proposed, or cheerfully agreed to, as a full reparation of personal damages, in consideration of the additional favor of a reversal of the attainders.

It seems to me impossible, after carefully pondering the whole story, not to feel that, more than the loss of lands and goods, the sufferers and survivors felt the loss of fellowship. Neighbors and kindred contemned them. Like the fruit of man's first disobedience, the curse laid upon them descended to their innocent posterity; and in some instances the sentence of ecclesiastical excommunication had filled their cup of woe by formally consigning the revered parent or the tenderly loved child, husband, or wife to sure and eternal damnation. These circumstances were likely to impress the survivors with a sense of infamy and utter desolation, to which any material loss were but as the stolen purse to Othello.

It is pleasant to know how fully the prayers of these petitioners for a restoration of their good name have been answered. Their descendants to-day, filling their full share of places of honor and trust,

"Hear no reproachful whispers on the wind,"

from the graves of their ancestors. The instigators of, and principal actors in, their persecution have sunk into comparative oblivion, or are remembered with aversion and contempt. On the other hand, almost the only sweet episodes in our memory of men and manners at that early day are to be found in the accounts which have been transmitted to us of the fortitude and composure with which those victims of irresponsible power endured the insane atrocities inflicted upon them, and the glimpses we there obtain of the mutual affection between the sufferers and those near and dear to them. The tender offices which their friends and kindred performed for them while living, and the efforts to remove the stigma of condemnation after they were dead, are as noble and disinterested deeds as have ever been commemorated in history or in song. Nothing else has withstood the ravages of time that better serves to show the susceptibility of the human heart to tenderest emotions, even amidst prevailing malevolence and superstition, and nowhere else can we perceive a ray of solace or of beauty in the painful details of that picture of early provincial life.

Dr. Moore finds support for his theory of the spuriousness of this copy in its "long concealment," which is strengthened by the fact that it has no known duplicate,— "one solitary printed copy." I confess I fail to see in these circumstances, taken separately or together, a foundation for a reasonable doubt; nor do I believe that he will insist that there is any recognized rule that requires the determination of the authenticity of prints supposed to be "unique," to be postponed until all doubt is removed by the discovery of other copies, or until the individual history of each shall have been traced, step by step, to the first possessor.

I venture to say that in his unrivalled collection of the Laws, and the Journals of the House of Representatives, of Massachusetts, our friend here must have pages — yes, and volumes even — that cannot be duplicated, which I am sure are, in his estimation, not less valuable on that account, either to the bibliophilist, the lawyer, or the historian. Whether other copies of this impression may hereafter appear, or not, is of no consequence when we consider that the printers might, with little extra labor, have pulled a score or a hundred sheets while the form was in the press. And who shall say that they did not?

Neither, since the antiquity of the paper is conceded, and it clearly appears to be of the typography of Bartholomew Green, do I think it material to trace its history in all the obscure past. It may be of interest, however, to know that this particular copy was purchased at the sale of the collection of the late J. K. Wiggin, and that it bears the autograph signature of Nathaniel Lambert, who in 1805 — when he appears to have signed it — was the ward, as well as the office-assistant of Ichabod Tucker, Clerk of the Courts and a successor of Stephen Sewall. This takes the paper back nearly half the period of its existence, through channels that apparently lead to no suspicious source. We may well question if it is possible to give as satisfactory an account of any of the numerous genuine early prints which every now and then are emerging from obscurity into the glare of great libraries or the more subdued light of collectors' cabinets.

The argument founded on the absence of the bill and engrossment from the rolls or archives becomes of still inferior force when we consider the numerous casualties, by fire and revolution, which all the papers, of equal age, now remaining in the Secretary's office, have escaped. The engrossments of three hundred and sixty-seven public acts and of seven private acts have disappeared from that office by some means or other, together with probably a still larger number of original bills. Now, if we are to understand Dr. Moore's quotation of a paragraph from a message of the House of Representatives to Governor Hutchinson in 1770 as offered in support of the proposition that the existence of every act is to be finally tested by comparison with the engrossment, I think I shall find no difficulty in getting his proposition excluded, on the ground that it is practically untenable. And if the quotation is not made for this purpose, I cannot see the relevancy or the force of the argument he would base upon it. It is true that all acts of the General Court were required by the charter to be under the Province seal; and that they were engrossed on parchment, and signed by the executive, is an undeniable fact; but to conclude, hence, that, if the parchment is lost or destroyed, the act is a nullity, would be asserting a novel doctrine and indicating a new method of repeal, the legality of which our friend should not allow to rest unsupported by unequivocal and overwhelming authority. Such a proposition, if established, would overturn the entire system of the common law, which is based upon lost statutes whose purport has been handed down, by tradition, in the courts.

Now, coming to the record evidence, I begin with the remark that it is fortunate that the necessities of the case do not require me to explain all the obscurities of the proceedings of the General Court relating to the passage of this act. There being no Journal of the House of Representatives in existence for that period, and the files being imperfect, we are obliged to rely mainly upon the journals of the Governor and Council, commonly known as the General Court Records, for our knowledge of the doings of either branch. The originals of these journals were consumed, with the Court House, in 1747; and the duplicate copies, subsequently made, do not exactly agree with each other in all respects, and may fail to contain some important passages originally entered. I give this as a possible explanation of the absence of any express mention of the Governor's approval of certain acts in 1711, though, as to the act we are considering, I still adhere to the conjecture I have already expressed. The anachronism which Dr. Moore notices in my statement that the act "had passed the several stages of legislation," will disappear if the time referred to by me is understood to be the time of the Secretary's "making up his records." I admit that my statement is obscure, and that my friend might very naturally have supposed that I was under the false impression that the passage to enactment preceded the adoption of the report. Such, however, is not the case ; and I fully concur in his criticism concerning the unsatisfactoriness of the record.

My statement was a deduction from my previous showing from the records, which I believe was full and accurate ; so there was, and is, no danger of being misled by it one way or the other ; nor, since Dr. Moore has so fully supplemented my work by his critical examination of the record entries, in his rejoinder, need we again go over the ground.

One suggestion here, however, will perhaps help to reconcile any apparent discrepancy between the report and the act, and account for the twofold proceedings.[1] The act began in the Council, where the tradition concerning the exclusive right of the Representatives to originate money-bills may have operated to the rejection of any clause requiring an appropriation. When the bill was returned from the House, it was not amended, or replaced by a new draught, but it was accompanied by an order, proposed in the House, providing for the compensation asked for, as well as for the appointment of a joint committee to ascertain the names of the persons who were to receive it. If, as is probable, the Representatives felt this to be the best course to pursue under the circumstances, the Council certainly could not object to it, since it left their bill intact, except in regard to one feature in which the co-operation of the House was expected as being necessary to perfect the bill.

[1] It may at the same time furnish a satisfactory answer to Dr. Moore's question, "Why was it that an act was not drawn embracing all the recommendations of the committee?" etc. Proc. Mass. Hist. Soc., vol. xxi. p. 87.

The declaration of the committee that the claims of the petitioners were "moderated," or abated, cannot be refuted by comparing the report with the claims on file, until we have ascertained that the latter were the first and only demands presented; which the very declaration renders doubtful, to say the least.

Again, the mystery of the omission from the act, of the names of seven of the persons condemned is not cleared up — at least so as to throw the responsibility upon the legislature — by the letter of Nehemiah Jewett to Major Sewall, which Dr. Moore has given us in full; because that letter bears the following indorsement, in Sewall's handwriting, "Mr Jewets note ab⁰ yᵉ psons condemned *and not returned to ye Gener^{ll} Court.*" This important memorandum, which is not printed by Woodward, leaves the question still open as to whether or not Jewett had any good reason for his supposition. Seeing that it was thus indecisive, I did not deem it worth while to comment upon it in my reply to Dr. Moore's Notes.

On one point, however, Dr. Moore has clearly convicted me of the very fault that I had animadverted upon in the conduct of the committee. I charged them with carelessness in not reporting the Christian name of Goodwife Corey. This is inexcusable, and I thank my friend for the correction. But though the illustration fails in this instance, the charge is equally well sustained by their omission to report the name of Thomas Rich, — Goodwife Corey's son by a former marriage. On referring to my notes, I find that this was the only omission I had intended to point out; but in the hurry of composition I was in this particular led into a misinterpretation of my brief minutes, probably by noticing that the Christian name of the mother did not appear either in the act or in the committee's list sent by Jewett to Sewall.[1] This mistake would not have occurred if I had made the slightest comparison of my notes with the report accepted by the legislature.

Having thus pondered the evidence which the act itself affords, and examined into the precedent and contemporaneous circumstances which the records disclose, let us resume the consideration of the extraneous evidence which Dr. Moore adduces to confirm his assertion that no such act was passed.

[1] Jewett, who acted as chairman of the committee, was probably responsible for the omission in the act, as it is very likely that he drew the bill.

We are pointed to the fact, as significant, that the Rev. Israel Loring, in 1737, and Governor Belcher, in 1740, appear to have had no knowledge of any such act. But this, if it proves anything, proves too much. It shows that these worthies were as ignorant that the sufferers had received compensation — which nobody disputes — as that the attainders had been reversed. If the force of the blow demolishes the one, it recoils with equal force upon the other; and either both the act and report are not affected by it, or they fall together.

It is indeed unaccountable that legislative proceedings of such importance should so soon pass out of memory; but the fact is, nevertheless, undeniable. And an instance even more striking than this is the utter failure of everybody concerned, — the committee, the several assemblies, and the petitioners themselves, — from 1708 to 1711, to take any notice of the act to reverse attainders, passed in 1703, which was only about five years before the proceedings were instituted that resulted in the passage of the present act.[1] Can our ingenious friend devise an explanation of this remarkable oversight that will not apply with equal or increased force to the forgetfulness manifested a generation later? This is one of the mysteries which I confess myself incompetent to solve. I feel reasonably sure, however, that the committee of 1750 *did* discover the facts relative to the compensation, and the reversal of the attainder. Hence it was — and not to justify a report that was never made, as my friend rashly concludes — that I expressed the opinion that it was their duty to report against reconsidering the claim: a duty from which they ought not to have been deterred by any considerations of pity for the "mean, low, and abject circumstances" to which the unfortunate descendants of the condemned had been reduced, and which — to his credit, be it said — moved good Parson Loring to sympathy and to efforts in their behalf.

If, after our friend shall have reviewed the subject in the aspect in which I now leave it, he shall not agree with me that the presumption that the act was regularly passed prevails over all the doubts and difficulties which, except for his shrewd insight and large knowledge, would perhaps never have obscured its title to recognition, I shall be disappointed;

[1] See Dr. Moore's comment on this, in his first note in Proc. Mass. Hist. Soc., vol. xxi. p. 88.

but in such case there is no one, I am sure, more likely than he to discover some further evidence so decisive that this shall no longer remain an exception to our uniform agreement on historical questions.

Meanwhile the inscription which my scholarly friend has suggested as proper to be placed on the cabinet wherein the "remains" of the act are deposited, must be for the present declined. As custodian of the relic, I feel that I ought to be better assured that it never had vitality before I entomb it under an epitaph.

If any inscription were necessary, I think the following would be more appropriate : —

Stat mole sua; nullus esse potest ambigendi locus.

This fragile leaf has survived five generations of men, to attest to the candid descendants of honorable ancestors, many of whose good deeds the world has forgotten — while the errors which they shared with their contemporaries have been loudly proclaimed — a singular instance of their justice and generosity, in that, while they were the first of all people to escape the thraldom of a superstition to which in Christian Europe alone it is estimated that more than nine millions of innocent human beings have been sacrificed, they were also the first to make pecuniary reparation to the descendants of those who had been ignorantly condemned for witchcraft; and then BY THIS INSTRUMENT they not only restored the forfeited estates of the victims, but rescued their names and the names of their posterity from perpetual infamy : AN ACT OF LEGISLATION, WITHOUT PRECEDENT OR PARALLEL, and which, though hitherto scarcely noticed, will grow more lustrous with the lapse of time.

" *So shines a good deed in a naughty world.*"

FURTHER NOTES

ON THE

HISTORY OF WITCHCRAFT IN MASSACHUSETTS,

CONTAINING

ADDITIONAL EVIDENCE OF THE PASSAGE OF THE

ACT OF 1711,

FOR REVERSING THE ATTAINDERS OF THE WITCHES;

ALSO, AFFIRMING THE LEGALITY

OF THE

SPECIAL COURT OF OYER AND TERMINER
OF 1692:

WITH A HELIOTYPE PLATE OF THE ACT OF 1711, AS PRINTED IN 1713,

AND

AN APPENDIX

OF DOCUMENTS, ETC.

BY

ABNER CHENEY GOODELL, JR.

REPRINTED, WITH SLIGHT ALTERATIONS, FROM THE PROCEEDINGS
OF THE MASSACHUSETTS HISTORICAL SOCIETY.

CAMBRIDGE:
JOHN WILSON AND SON.
University Press.
1884.

WITCH-TRIALS IN MASSACHUSETTS.

AT the annual meeting of the American Antiquarian Society, last October, our corresponding associate, Mr. George H. Moore, read an elaborate paper upon some features of the History of Witchcraft in Massachusetts,* leading to the following conclusions: first, that Hutchinson, Chalmers, and others who have followed them, are wrong in asserting that at the time of the indictments for witchcraft, in 1692, there was no law of the colony or province in force, against witchcraft; second, that the often-repeated statement that no lawyer was engaged in the proceedings, is equally erroneous; third, that the act reversing "the several convictions, judgments, and attainders against the persons executed, and several who were condemned but not executed," which has been frequently referred to as having been passed by the general court, never became a law; and, fourth, that the several attempts by the legislature, to make adequate pecuniary compensation to the persons attainted, in the trials for witchcraft, or to their representatives, appear to have been abortive; or, to quote the concluding paragraph of his appendix, "'the cry of the long-oppressed sufferers,' seems to have been stifled: at any rate, it was heard no more in the high places of legislation."

If either of these conclusions is unsound, it cannot be too promptly challenged, for I think it will not be denied that few persons, living or dead, have studied the history of the early legislation of Massachusetts more assiduously and intelligently than has Mr. Moore, that his knowledge of our legislative bibliography is unsurpassed, and that, *prima facie*, his statements relating thereto deserve implicit credit. I confess that I entirely agree with him in his first and second conclusions, and I acknowledge my obligation to him for thus venturing to correct what seem to me to be important errors;

---

* Proc. Am. Antiq. Soc., p. 162 *et seq.*

but from his third and fourth conclusions, most reluctantly, I feel it my duty to express dissent, to which I am compelled, in part, by a consideration of facts not referred to either in his article or in the appendix; and the chief purpose of what I shall now offer is to give my reasons for this dissent.

Moreover, while I concur in Mr. Moore's opinion that the colony law against witchcraft was in force in 1692,* I nevertheless deem it due to Hutchinson to admit that there are, in a certain aspect, fairly, two sides to the question; and that the opinion he expresses coincides with that of most of the legal minds of his day, as well as with the views of the advisers of the crown to whom were submitted the acts of the first provincial legislature. And, again, with all deference to Mr. Moore, it does not seem to me to be necessary to argue from general principles that the laws of the colony survived the constitutional and administrative changes between the time of the forfeiture of the colonial charter and the organization of the provincial government; for we have in the commissions and ordinances of Dudley and Andros, and in the declaration of the subsequent revolutionary government, — which was substantially ratified by the letter of King William, — successive express sanctions of all former legislation not repugnant to the laws of England.† Even the province charter, which, it is true, does not, in express terms, ratify or continue former laws, does so, impliedly, in the clause relating to taxes, which are therein directed to be disposed of "according to such acts as *are*, or shall be, in force within our said Province."

We are, therefore, I think, saved the labor of nice inquiry into the validity of the judgment against the charter, on *quo warranto*, and into the legal effect of political revolution upon the municipal laws, and even into the question of how far the judicial proceedings against the persons accused of witchcraft were justified by the common law, since, under all administrations, the only colony laws abrogated — except such as were expressly repealed — were those that were repugnant to the laws of England, in which class the colonial act against witchcraft was not properly included.

Now this question of repugnancy, as I understand it, should be the only point of divergence between those who, with Hutchinson, affirm that this law of the colony was obsolete, and those who, with Mr. Moore, declare that it was in force. I repeat, therefore, that I coincide with Mr. Moore, not

---

* See Appendix A., *infra*. † *Ibid.*

because this law was a part of the municipal code which, on general principles, survived all perturbations of the state, but because I fail to see that there was an essential repugnancy between the colonial and parliamentary acts. The statute of 1 James I. ch. 12, it is true, contained a clause saving her dower to the widow, and the inheritance to the heir, for the want of which, ostensibly, the provincial act of Dec. 14, 1692,* — which was intended to follow, substantially, the English statute,—was rejected by the privy council; but this clause would have been superfluous in the provincial act, inasmuch as the "Act setting forth General Privileges," passed Oct. 13, 1692, to which Mr. Moore refers, had already provided that "all lands and heritages within this province shall be free from all . . . escheats and forfeitures upon the death of parents or ancestors, natural, casual, or judicial, and that forever, except in cases of high treason." † Taking the husband to be the ancestor, that is, the *antecessor*, of the widow, this would have saved her dower, as well as the inheritance. In this view of the case, the reasons alleged by the privy council for rejecting the act are insufficient.

It is to be observed that the "repugnancy" which — though in this instance consisting only in a variance between the provincial act and the parliamentary model — was deemed fatal, was not assigned as a reason for disallowing the clause against witchcraft in the act of Oct. 29, 1692,‡ which was copied verbatim from the old law of the colony. Witchcraft was felony by the statute of James, and though the pretended practice of some forms of it was visited with less severe penalties in England than in this province, it is far from clear that, therefore, the statutes denouncing these severer penalties were "repugnant" to the act of James, according to the obvious purport of that word in the charter. If difference in degree or kind of punishment constitutes a fatal repugnance, what shall be said of the generality of the punitive laws of the province, which were notoriously at variance with the barbarous criminal legislation of the mother country? There

---

* 1692-93, chap. 40, and note.
† 1692-93, chap. 11. This provision was, substantially, the tenth article of the colonial declaration of rights, or Body of Liberties of 1641 (see Mass. Hist. Coll., 3d series, vol. viii. p. 218), and was continued under the title "Lands" in the editions of the colony laws of 1660 and 1672, with a slight verbal change. It differed from the provincial act mainly in extending the exemption from forfeiture, to the case of treason. It may be questioned if this exemption did not render the colonial ordinance "repugnant to the laws of England" within the meaning of the charter; since the effect of it was to deprive the crown, in a part of its dominions, of a most ancient and important branch of revenue.
‡ 1692-93, chap. 19.

seems to be no reason why repugnancy may not consist in falling below as well as in exceeding the standard; and yet this objection was never made, on that account, to any act of our provincial legislature.

The objection to the provincial statute of December 14, appears to have been to its want of substantial conformity to all the provisions of the original pattern. This objection was special, and did not extend beyond the particular act in question. The objections to the earlier act, of October 29, were twofold: first, that the crime was too indefinitely stated; and, second, that, contrary to the common law, the offence was made capital; and this — notwithstanding that the usual purpose of statutory enactment is to change the common law — was the only repugnance suggested. It seems to have been agreed among the court lawyers of that period that, to avoid repugnancy, an act of the provincial legislature against witchcraft should either strictly define the offence and treat it as a misdemeanor, according to the common law, or, if it declared the offence capital, that it should conform substantially to all the provisions of the existing act of parliament. However ingenious and satisfactory their reasons for this conclusion may have been deemed one or two centuries ago, these reasons will hardly prove convincing to the modern mind, whether lay or professional, accustomed to interpret words according to their intended purport rather than according to any literal or technical construction that may be put upon them.

As to the second conclusion, Mr. Moore has done no more than justice to the character of Newton as a lawyer, and has sufficiently refuted the statement that lawyers had nothing to do with the witch-trials. If he had gone further, and accorded to Stoughton extraordinary attainments in legal learning, he would, I think, have been fully sustained by what the records of our early legislation and jurisprudence attest of this singularly able man, who, notwithstanding the character which has been given to him of an "atrabilious old bachelor," seems not to have neglected that "jealous mistress" — the common law — who, it is said, "must lie alone." It is true that he, as well as Dudley and Sewall, was bred a clergyman; but those who imagine that the study of divinity unfits the student for forensic, legislative, or magisterial duties are to be reminded that the legal is but a lay branch of the clerical profession from which it sprung; and that the secularizing of jurisprudence is a work of modern times, not yet completed. If divines sometimes took to the law, lawyers, from time immemorial, quite as often dabbled in divinity, and that not alone in Doctors-Commons. Even Checkley, the apothecary, has had notable successors in the office of attorney-general, who would have shown less skill in dealing with the novel and perplexing difficulties of that office, and certainly not a better understanding than he manifested of the criminal law as then generally administered.

To mention the special profession of an individual or class as necessarily a disqualification for efficient service in a different capacity comes very near to sneering. The proper course would be to compare the career of the person criticised, by the standard of that of others in the same employment; and in that case, I think, the three magistrates I have named, each of whom acceptably held the post — either in Massachusetts or New York — of chief justice of the highest judicial court, will compare favorably, in respect to all those acquirements necessary to the proper conduct of trials and the administering of forensic justice, as well as to the management of the higher affairs of state, with, at least, the average benchers of the inns of court in the days of William and Anne. Upon Stoughton, especially, fell the responsible task not only of piloting the ship of state, just launched under the new charter, and of acting as the legal adviser of a governor confessedly dependent upon him for all knowledge of the law and of legal procedure,* but of devising a system of judicature and forms of judicial proceedings that have continued substantially unchanged for nearly two centuries.† The regret which some — in consequence of the representations of late writers upon the witch-trials — may have been led to feel that those trials had not been conducted by lawyers, is not warranted by the disclosures of the records of the tribunals of England or her colonies, if it springs from the belief that a more humane and rational course of procedure might, in that case, have been expected. While it would be unjust to charge upon Newton the sole responsibility for the results of the witch-trials of 1692, or even for the manner in which those trials were conducted, — the admission of spectre evidence, the assumption that the accused were guilty, the inducements used to extort confessions, and the menaces against those who denied their guilt (all of which he must at

---

* See extract from Phips's letter to Nottingham, Feb. 20, 1692: Prov. Laws, vol. i. p. 107.

† See the laws passed in Stoughton's administration, *passim*. He was during this time, also, chief justice of the Superior Court of Judicature, and Judge of Probate for Suffolk, whence issued all the precedents of probate forms. Undoubtedly he received assistance from others; but there is merit in knowing how to select good advisers.

least have approved of or connived at),—the candid student of those so-called trials will not fail to notice that it was not until after this thoroughbred lawyer had been superseded as prosecuting attorney that the juries began to acquit.

Against Mr. Moore's third conclusion, I not only assert confidently that the act for reversing attainders was actually passed, but I offer to the Society, for our Proceedings, the use of heliotype plates of the act itself, printed, in 1713, by "B. Green, Printer to His Excellency the Governour and Council."

As I am partly responsible for Mr. Moore's opinion that this act was never passed, and as he has not traced the progress of the attempts that were made to enact it, which he supposes to have been abortive, I will endeavor to give, in full, from the records, the legislative proceedings for compensating the sufferers, and to follow the progress of this act from the inceptive petition to its final passage.

From a word and figure, cancelled in the following petition, it appears that it was prepared to be presented at the October session, 1708; and, by another cancelled word, it appears that the petitioners were not all willing to profess their belief that the judges and jurors did what they thought was right, in that "hour of Darkness." The petition was presented to the Council, in the May session of 1709, and is as follows:—

"To his Excelency the Gouenor and ye Honarable Counsell and Genarall Asembly for ye Prouince of ye Massatusetts Bay in New England Conuen,d at Boston ~~October~~ May 25th 1709

The Humble Adress and motion of Seueral of ye Inhabitants of ye sd Prouince some of which had their near Relations Either Parents or others who suffered Death in ye Dark and Dollful times y^t past ouer this prouince in ye Year 1692 under ye suposition and in y^t Gloumy Day by some (thought prou,d) of Being Guilty of wichcraft wch we haue all ye Reson in ye world to hope and beleiue they were Inocent off. and others of us y^t Either our selues or some of our Relations haue Been Imprison'd impared and Blasted in our Reputations and Estates by Reson of ye same, its not our Intent Neither Do we Reflect on ye Judges or Jurors Concern^d in those Sorrowfull tryals whome we hope ~~and Beleiue~~ Did y^t wch they thought was Right in y^t hour of Darkness. but y^t wch we moue and pray for is y^t You Would Pleas to pass some sutable Act as in Your Wisdom You may think meet and proper y^t shall (so far as may be) Restore ye Reputations to ye Posterity of ye suffurers and Remunerate them as to what they haue been Damnified in their Estates therby we Do not Without Remors and greif Recount these sorrowfull things But we Humbly Conceiue y^t we are Bound in Consience and Duty to god and to our-

Regni ANNÆ Reginæ Decimo.

Province of the Massachusetts-Bay.

AN ACT.

Made and Passed by the Great and General Court or Assembly of Her Majesty's Province of the Massachusetts Bay in New-England, Held at Boston the 17th Day of October, 1711.

An Act to Reverse the Attainders of George Burroughs and others for Witchcraft.

FORASMUCH as in the Year of our Lord One Thousand Six Hundred Ninety Two, Several Towns within this Province were Infested with a horrible Witchcraft or Possession of Devils ; And at a Special Court of Oyer and Terminer holden at Salem, in the County of Essex in the same Year One Thousand Six Hundred Ninety Two, George Burroughs of Wells, John Procter, George Jacob, John Willard, Giles Core, and his Wife, Rebecca Nurse, and Sarah Good, all of Salem aforesaid: Elizabeth How of Ipswich; Mary Eastey, Sarah Wild and Abigail Hobbs all of Topsfield : Samuel Wardell, Mary Parker, Martha Carrier, Abigail Falkner, Anne Foster, Rebecca Eames, Mary Post, and Mary Lacey, all of Andover : Mary Bradbury of Salisbury : and Dorcas Hoar of Beverly ; Were severally Indicted, Convicted and Attained of Witchcraft, and some of them put to Death, Others lying still under the like Sentence of the said Court, and liable to have the same Executed upon them.

A   The

Anno Regni ANNÆ Reginæ Decimo.

The Influence and Energy of the Evil Spirits so great at that time acting in and upon those who were the Principal Accusers and Witnesses, proceeding so far as to cause a Prosecution to be had of Persons of known and good Reputation, which caused a great Dissatisfaction and a stop to be put thereunto, until Their Majesties Pleasure should be known therein.

And upon a Representation thereof accordingly made, Her late Majesty Queen *MARY* the Second, of blessed Memory, by Her Royal Letter given at Her Court at *Whitehall* the Fifteenth of *April* 1693. was Graciously Pleas'd to approve the Care and Circumspection therein; and to Will and Require that in all proceedings against Persons Accused for Witchcraft, or being Possessed by the Devil, the greatest Moderation, and all due Circumspection be Used, so far as the same may be without Impediment to the ordinary Course of Justice.

And some of the Principal Accusers and Witnesses in those dark and severe Prosecutions have since discovered themselves to be Persons of Profligate and Vicious Conversation.

Upon the humble Petition and Suit of several of the said Persons, and of the Children of others of them whose Parents were Executed.

Be it Declared and Enacted by His Excellency the Governour, Council and Representatives, in General Court Assembled, and by the Authority of the same, That the several Convictions, Judgments and Attainders against the said *George Burroughs, John Procter, George Jacob, John Willard, Giles Core,* and _____ *Core, Rebecca Nurse, Sarah Good, Elizabeth How, Mary Eastey, Sarah Wild, Abigail Hobbs, Samuel Wardell, Mary Parker, Martha Carrier, Abigail Falkner, Anne Foster, Rebecca Eames, Mary Post, Mary Lacey, Mary Bradbury* and *Dorcas Hoar,* and every of them, Be and hereby are Reversed, Made and Declared to be Null and Void to all Intents, Constructions and Purposes whatsoever, as if no such Convictions, Judgments or Attainders had ever been had or given. And that no Penalties or Forfeitures of Goods or Chattels be by the said Judgments and Attainders, or either of them had or incurr'd.

Any Law, Usage or Custom to the contrary notwithstanding.

And that no Sheriff, Constable, Goaler, or other Officer shall be liable to any Prosecution in the Law for any thing they then Legally did in the Execution of their respective Offices.

BOSTON: Printed by *B. Green*, Printer to His Excellency the GOVERNOUR and COUNCIL. 1713.

selues Relatiues and posterity and Country Humbly to make this Motion praying God to Direct You in this and all Your Weighty Consultations. —

We subscribe Your sorrowfull and Distrest Supliants

PHILIP ENGLISH
ISACK ESTEY sen
BENIAMIN PROCTER
JOHN PROCTER
THORNDIK PROCTER
GEORGE JACOBS
WILLIAM BUCKLY
IOHN NURS

JOHN TARBELL
JOHN PARKER
JOSEPH PARKER
JOHN JOHNSON
FRANCIS FAULKNER

ISAAC ESTEY
JOSEPH ESTY
S^AMUEL NURS
BE^NIAMIN NURS
JOHN PRESTON
SAMUEL NURS iu
WILLIAM RUSELL
FRANCIS NURS
GEORG NURS "*

The following votes were thereupon passed: —

Petition of Isaac Easty &c "Thursday June 9, 1709. . . . Upon Reading a Petition of Isaac Easty John Nurse &c in Behalf of themselves & divers others, who themselves or their Relations were prosecuted in the Time of the Witchcraft in 1692, Praying to be restored to their Reputation, And to be Remunerated what they have been damaged in their Estates;

Order thereon. Ordered that a Bill be brought in for Restoring them accordingly." †

Bill for Reversing attaind's for Witchcraft. "Fryday, June 10, 1709. . . . A Bill to Reverse the Attainders of several Persons for Witchcraft. Read three several Times Debated & Pass'd: — The Names of the Persons to be inserted by the Agreement of both Houses." ‡

What debates ensued upon the introduction of this subject can only be imagined. It is to be inferred that the feeling in the Council that the attainders should be reversed, and some pecuniary reparation made to the sufferers or their representatives, was general. Stoughton, who never repented of his connection with the trials, had been dead eight years; and the Mathers, though still professing unshaken belief in demonology, had long adopted the prevalent opinion that the Devil could assume the shape of innocence, and they had not withstood the reaction, which had become almost universal, in favor of some, if not all, of the accused; and their opinions,

---

* Mass. Archives, cxxxv. p. 125.
† Council Records, vol. viii. p. 454. These records are improperly marked "General Court Records," but they are, strictly, the legislative records of the governor and council. The series referred to is that belonging to the State Library except when otherwise designated.
‡ *Ibid.*, pp. 454, 455.

though not so authoritative as formerly, were still of great weight even in "high places."

The bill that was reported, or "brought in" under the order just mentioned, was, undoubtedly, identical with the act which was finally passed, except that it did not contain the names of the persons attainted. Having reached this stage it seems to have been dropped, for the session; but, from the following entry, it appears that it was revived at the October session, and sent to the representatives, for their concurrence: —

"Wednesday, Nov. 9, 1709. . . . A Bill pass'd at the Session of this Court in May last for Reversing the Attainders of . . . . Arraign'd & Convicted of Witchcraft, was again Read Voted to be Revived & sent down for Concurrence." *

What followed the passage of this vote, during that year, appears only in the vote of Oct. 27, 1711, hereafter given; for the House, at that time, did not print its journals, and there is no other known record of the separate doings of the representatives. In the vote referred to, the bill is declared to have been passed to its engrossment by the House in 1709; but whether at the October or February session does not appear: probably at the former. During the first session of the next year the bill thus passed by the House reappears in the Council, and the following entry shows that, with it, the House sent up an order for a joint committee to complete the bill by inserting the names of the persons attainted, and to ascertain and report what money should be allowed to them or to their respective representatives in compensation for their losses in the witchcraft persecutions, and that this committee was appointed: —

"Tuesday, June 27, 1710. . . . A Bill pass'd in both Houses for Reversing the Attainders of Persons condemned for Witchcraft in the Year 1692: left Blank for Inserting the Names of the several Persons;

Voted a Concurrence with the Representatives on the following Order annex'd thereto; viz, — Ordered that John Burrill, Nehemiah Jewett Esq^{rs} & Mr James Barns with such as the Honble Board shall appoint be a Committee to Inquire into the Names to be inserted into the Bill, & what Damages they sustained by their Prosecutions & make Report to this Court; And John Appleton & Thomas Noyes Esq^{rs} nominated to be of the s^d Comm^{tee}." †

---

* Council Records, vol. viii. p. 508.

† Ibid., vol. ix. p. 49. In this instance I have copied from the series in the Secretary's Office; the entry there being more complete and evidently more correct.

No further traces of the bill have been found in the records, until the fifth legislative session of the next year, when the following entry occurs : —

"Oct. 27, 1711. A Bill for reversing the Attainders of George Burroughs & others for Witchcraft, pass'd by the General Assembly at their Sessions 1709, to be Engross'd ; & a Committee to consider the Names of Persons to be inserted, & upon their Report now inserted, was again read & Pass'd to be engross'd." *

This bill had been kept alive by virtue of a general order passed the last day of the second session of 1711 continuing all unfinished business to the fall session. It was now again passed to be engrossed in its complete form.

Let us now inquire into the doings of the committee to whom the bill was intrusted by the vote of June 27, 1710.

After notice to the petitioners and all others supposed to be interested, this committee met at Pratt's Tavern in Salem, on the 13th of September following their appointment,† and seem to have found the business of preparing a list of the names of the persons attainted and of ascertaining the amount of compensation that would be satisfactory to the claimants, so far advanced that they were able to agree upon and sign a report the next day.‡ This report is the same that was accepted by the General Court in October, 1711, after slumbering somewhere for more than a year.

An examination of the court files, at Salem, furnishes a probable explanation of this expedition on the part of the committee. Soon after their report was accepted, Major Stephen Sewall, who had been the clerk of the Special Court of Oyer and Terminer, and who still continued to hold the office of clerk of the courts in Essex County, was appointed, by a large majority of the claimants to whom damages were awarded, to act for them in the business of collecting the same from the province treasurer.§ Nothing is more likely than that he, having the custody of the records of the court, and, doubtless, well remembering the persons and circumstances connected with the trials, had not only solicited the appointment of attorney, but had been active in helping

---

* Council Records, vol. ix. p. 136.

† Their original report bears date Sept. 14, 1710, but the record gives it one year later, which was but little more than one month before it was acted upon by the General Court. The former, however, is undoubtedly the correct date.

‡ See Appendix D. The original report, printed in Mr. Moore's appendix correctly, except with the omission of the date, does not show the recorded signature of Dudley approving of the resolve.

§ S e Appendix B.

along the suit for redress, from the beginning, and had thus been able to prepare and lay before the committee the list, which, coming from so trustworthy a source, and not being objected to, was adopted by them without further inquiry. This attorneyship of Major Sewall was not performed gratuitously; and the emoluments arising from it were, no doubt, a tempting inducement to one who got his living, largely, from official fees established upon a more moderate scale.

It is not a little surprising to find, after the agitation of this subject before the legislature had continued so long, and after the committee had had such ample opportunity, both as to time and evidence, that the names of seven persons clearly within the intention of the act, were overlooked and omitted. Some of them probably had not retained the services of the clerk; and the committee ascertained their names when it was too late to secure for them the benefit of the act, and a share in the appropriation; but the omission of others requires further explanation than the records furnish.*

The committee marshalled the claimants into three classes: first, the representatives of those who were executed; second, those who were condemned but not executed; and, third, those who suffered imprisonment but were not condemned.† To the first two classes they awarded the full sum finally claimed by each. The amounts reported were, to be sure, in some instances, somewhat less than the statement of loss first exhibited by the claimants; but, upon conference with the committee, the respective demands, it appears, were "moderated," to the mutual satisfaction of the claimants and the committee.‡ The claims of the third class were wholly rejected, as not being within the purview of the order of the General Court. The demand of Philip English, who suffered enormous damage, but whose claim for compensation rested

---

* The names omitted are Bridget Bishop, Susanna Martin, Alice Parker, Ann Pudeator, Wilmot Read, Margaret Scott and Elizabeth Johnson, Junior. Abigail Faulkner, Sarah Wardwell, and Elizabeth Procter had already been exonerated by the act of 1703, which Mr. Moore has given us in full, and accurately collated, in his appendix. The reasons for including either of them in the present act are not obvious. Mrs. Wardwell's son Samuel applied to have her name inserted, but I have discovered no such effort in behalf of Mrs. Procter. Mr. Upham does not include Elizabeth Johnson's name among those that were omitted; but she was attainted, and formally applied to the committee for the benefit of the act. Her petition, however, came too late. Her attainder therefore still remains unreversed. See note † p. 17, *infra.*

† See Appendix C.
‡ See Appendix D.

upon peculiar grounds, hereafter explained, was not passed upon by the committee, but reserved for the future consideration of the General Court.*

We have now reached the record of the passage of the bill to be enacted, which is as follows: —

"Nov. 2, 1711. The engross'd Bill to reverse the Attenders of George Borroughs & others for Witchcraft; Pass'd in the House of Represent^{ves}. Read & Concur'd to be Enacted." †

Here we encounter a doubt which cannot be wholly removed without reference to external evidence. While the record is express as to the enactment, it does not show that the bill was signed by the governor. Did the governor sign the bill?

I have acknowledged my share of responsibility for Mr. Moore's conclusion that the act for reversing attainders, &c., never became a law; ‡ I did so, inasmuch as the absence of the title of this act from the edition of the Province Laws now being printed by the State was, I am informed, regarded by him as a conclusive confirmation of the result of his inquiries upon the subject in other directions. The story of this omission is as follows: —

The care of compiling and editing the materials collected by the Commissioners on the Province Laws was, by the indulgence of my learned associate, intrusted solely to me, who alone am responsible for whatever avoidable errors the work contains. When, in the course of this labor, I reached the year 1711, I found the titles of several acts recorded in the legislative records of the Council as passed that year, which did not appear, from any evidence immediately accessible, to have been signed by the governor and sealed with the province seal. I, therefore, in a note,§ ventured to express the opinion that probably they were never enacted. But, before the book had gone to the bindery, I received from Mr. Sainsbury, who previously had searched the Public Record Office in vain for any evidence of the passage of these acts, copies of three of them, which will be found in the postscript appended to the volume alluded to; and a fourth act, completing the list, was generously furnished the Commissioners by Mr. Moore, to whom they are indebted not only for ready assistance on all occasions, but for the most hearty and appre-

---

* See p. 17, *infra*, and Appendix C.
† Council Records, vol. ix. p. 140.
‡ *Supra*, p. 8. § Province Laws, vol. i. p. 686.

ciative encouragement. It is in view of these facts that I claim a share in whatever censure that indefatigable scholar may have incurred by relying too implicitly upon my incautious expressions.

The copy of the printed act for reversing the attainders, which is believed to be unique, is not the only evidence, besides the entry last quoted from the records, of the passage of the act; for the record further shows that Dudley consented to the vote accepting the report of the names to be inserted in the act.* As this report supplied all that was wanting to make the bill, which had passed the several stages of legislation, complete and ready for the executive approval, it is not unlikely that the secretary of the province, in making up his records, supposed that this minute of the governor's assent to it was tantamount to the special entry of consent which was generally, but not always, written either immediately after the record of the vote of the passage of the bill to be enacted, or with the list of approved acts sometimes placed at the end of the record of the session.†

This act having been passed and the required sum appropriated, a warrant in due form, for drawing the money from the treasury, was issued by the secretary and signed by the governor, December 17, 1711.‡

In regard to the fourth and final conclusion which Mr. Moore apparently draws from his examination of the subject, it seems to me that he has overlooked the fact that the "payments of money" which, he says, "appear to have been made to various parties interested," — amounting in the whole to the very considerable sum of £578 12s., — were

---

* Council Records, vol. ix. p. 134. And see Appendix D, *infra*.

† As further evidence that the act was passed, we have the declaration to that effect of those who united in appointing Stephen Sewall to collect the compensation awarded to them by the committee, in 1711 (Appendix B), and also their request that he procure a copy of the act. From this copy, which is in the handwriting of Secretary Addington, and which — agreeing almost exactly with the act as printed in 1713 — still remains on the court files at Salem, Woodward had the impression made to which Mr. Moore alludes. Nor is this the only contemporaneous mention of the act to be found in the records; for Samuel Wardwell, in his petition in behalf of his mother (Feb. 19, 1711–12), declares that her "name is not inserted in the late Act of the General Court, for the taking off the Attainder of those that were condemned;" and Elizabeth Johnson, junior, in her petition (of the same date), after stating that the General Court "hath lately made an Act for taking off the Attainder of those that were condemned for witchcraft in the year 1692," represents that her name "is not inserted in said act," and prays that, if possible, it may be so inserted. See these petitions on file in the clerk's office, or as printed by Woodward, vol. ii. pp. 242, 243.

‡ A copy of this original warrant, in the handwriting of Stephen Sewall, remains on the court files at Salem, and is given in Appendix E.

not accepted merely as a compromise of larger claims, but were intended to be a fair equivalent for the forfeitures, fines, and amercements of those who were attainted; and that the amounts were amicably ascertained and fully agreed to, as such, upon a conference between the claimants and the committee.* The attainders appearing to have been unfounded, and the proceedings thereupon unjust to the accused, it was a noble and generous act of the legislature, however long postponed, to restore the whole of what, though forcibly taken from the accused, had enured to the crown, for the use of the province, under the forms of law, and in strict accordance with the established practice in cases of felony, and for which, therefore, the petitioners had no legal redress. The amount thus repaid from the public treasury exceeded one fortieth of the province tax for the previous year, which, itself, was one of a series of necessary exactions unusually burdensome on account of the extraordinary expenses of Queen Anne's war in which the province took so important a part.†

Our sympathy for the sufferers should not lead us into the opposite injustice of condemning the legislature for not laying upon the people — those who were opposed to, as well as those who incited and approved of, the proceedings at Salem — a pecuniary burden which it had no moral right to impose. Even in the present enlightened age no legislature in Christendom would for a moment lend a favorable ear to the supplications for pecuniary redress, of persons who had been legally imprisoned on criminal charges, and subse-

---

* The book of records of the Court of Oyer and Terminer, if there ever was one, is not known to be in existence. In such a book, or the minutes or docket thereof, we should expect to find the originals of the estreats of fines, forfeitures, &c. It is possible that the estreats may be preserved elsewhere; but I have not seen them, and therefore assume that the amounts of damages found by the committee substantially agree with the amount found by the judicial authorities, upon proper inquiry in each case of attainder. See Appendix C.

† This grant to the sufferers was not the only pecuniary burden to which the public was subjected by this expensive folly. The records of the Superior Court contain an order passed at a session held, by adjournment at Salem, Dec. 12, 1692, approving of a schedule of expenses amountin to £130 0s. 11d., and ordering the court of sessions to lay an assessment therefor upon the county, which was done accordingly. Copies of the schedule and of the order to the court of sessions remain on the court files at Salem, and have been printed by Woodward. In addition to this sum to be assessed, two grants were made by the legislature in 1692, — one of £40 to Stephen Sewall, the clerk of the Court of Oyer and Terminer, for necessary charges of the court, and another to Mrs. Mary Gedney, innkeeper, for entertainment of the magistrates, jurors, and officers of the court. These, with the later grants to English and Rich, and the expenses of the various legislative committees, amount to a total of £1046 7s. 2d.

quently acquitted, or discharged as innocent. And however much we may wish that all the unhappy victims of that terrible infatuation had received ample recompense for loss of time and property, to say nothing of mental and physical suffering, and the social deprivations attending virtual outlawry, and however hard it may seem that the petitioners should have been denied, there can be no question that the course of the committee, with regard to the rejected claims, was in precise accordance with the universal practice of the present day.

That the committee performed their duty hastily and perfunctorily appears by the omission, from the act for reversing the attainders, of the names of some of the principal sufferers, as already noticed. It is further shown by other circumstances, — notably by their failure to ascertain the Christian name of Goodwife Corey, which appears in the files of the court, and which was known to her husband's children, who were among the petitioners for redress. Through the negligence of the committee in another particular, Thomas Rich became a supplicant to the legislature for compensation, as late as 1723, as Mr. Moore has shown in the carefully collated extracts from the records, which he has printed in the appendix to his article. Rich was the only surviving son of Goodwife Corey by a former husband; and the Corey family who received compensation in 1711 were not her children, but the children of Giles Corey by a former wife, or wives. When, therefore, upon the petition of Rich, these facts were made plain to the legislature, years afterwards, the House of Representatives, anxious to do equal justice to all for whom compensation was intended, made him a grant of £50, as the proper representative of this unfortunate woman; and this grant does not appear to be less than he claimed or expected.

The descendants of George Burroughs, however, whose supplementary memorial Mr. Moore also prints, had no proper claim. The legislature, in 1711, awarded to the widow and other representatives of that excellent and truly pious victim of superstition, the sum of £50 — that being the entire amount of their own estimate of their direct damage, and all they asked for. This was apportioned among them, at the time, evidently to the satisfaction of all, as the receipts on file show.* It is not too harsh to say that it was

---

* There was some dispute between the children of the former wives of Burroughs and his widow — who had been married to one Hall and took her own child with her to her new home — as to the equity of the apportionment, but the dispute seems to have been ended by the final award of the committee. See the receipts in Appendix F, from the court files in Salem, — inaccurately printed by Woodward.

the duty of the committee, in 1750, to report against reconsidering a claim thus fairly settled, and the reopening of which would have furnished a precedent for a general and formidable assault upon the province treasury.*

The failure of the committee to report any allowance, in the cases of Bridget Bishop and Elizabeth Johnson, which were clearly brought to their notice, is unaccountable. Whatever may have been their reasons for the omission, however, the fault is not chargeable to the province, or to the legislature, as a body.† It nowhere appears that the claim of any alleged sufferer was unheeded by the general court down to the time of the last application in the enlightened period of the administration of Shirley and Phips.‡

Philip English's case has been mentioned as exceptional.§ I have said that the committee did not include his claim among those adjusted by them, but referred his application to the special consideration of the general court.‖ As compensation for the damage suffered by him, the legislature voted him, as late as Nov. 10, 1718, the sum of £200 in full satis-

* The memorialists were probably encouraged by the spirit of liberality, not to say extravagance, prevailing in those flush times when the ruinous collapse of an inflated paper currency had been prevented by large remittances of silver from England in reimbursement of the expenses of the operations against Cape Breton. I will add as an item of possible interest, in this connection, that while neither the records nor the papers preserved in the court files show how Thomas Newman, Abiah Holbrook, and Elias Thomas — the memorialists in 1749 — were descended from their abused ancestor, there is little doubt that Thomas was the son of Peter Thomas, who married Elizabeth, the daughter of Rev. George Burroughs, and was, therefore, the uncle of Isaiah Thomas, the founder of the American Antiquarian Society.

† It does not appear that claims presented in 1711, on account of any other sufferers, were rejected. The claim of Edward Bishop, who estimated his total damage — remote and consequential, as well as direct — at £100, was classed by the committee with those of " persons imprisoned and not condemned," which, as has been said, were wholly excluded. It is possible that none of his wife's property was forfeited, which would account for the fact that no compensation was awarded to her representatives. This may also have been the case with Elizabeth Johnson, junior, whose brother Francis was a petitioner; but that these and so many others were omitted from the act seems insufficiently explained by the supposition that they were forgotten. See *ante*, note * p. 12.

‡ Notwithstanding the intimation by Oldmixon which Mr. Moore has quoted, that the province was beginning, as late as 1741, to repair the "mistake" of 1692, and Hutchinson's insinuation that sufficient compensation was not made (1st ed., vol. ii. p. 62, *n.*), Chalmers, with greater show of reason, on the very page from which Mr. Moore quotes his statement that there existed no law in Massachusetts for putting supposed witches to death, remarks : " The Assembly, however, did justice to the colony and to individuals when at the distance of twenty years it granted to the defendants [descendants?] of the innocent sufferers a compensation for the loss of their estates ; since they could not restore the lives which the present frenzy had taken away." — *Coll. N. Y. Hist. Soc.*, vol. i. p. 111.

§ See *ante*, p. 12. ‖ See Appendix C.

faction.* From the schedule of losses presented by him to the committee, at Salem, it appears that they amounted to £1183 2s., on account of what he " had seized, taken away, lost and embezzled" while he was in prison and during his flight, exclusive of the value of household goods and other chattels of which he was despoiled, and which he could not specify. As, after his arrest, he had been admitted to bail in the sum of £4000, and as neither he nor his wife was convicted, he claimed that whatever property was sequestrated by the sheriff was unlawfully taken.†

It is difficult if not impossible at this day, owing to the scandalous condition into which the records and files of the ancient courts in Suffolk have fallen, and in which they are still suffered to remain, to ascertain what proceedings, if any, were had against English on account of his flight, or what was the condition of the bond he gave for his liberation; but the law, loose and uncertain as it was, in most matters relating to proceedings against felons, seems, at that time, to have been so far settled as to have justified him in holding the sheriff accountable, as a trespasser, to the extent of his interference with the goods of the fugitive, beyond what was necessary to inventory them, before the flight was judicially ascertained; while, on the other hand, it is equally clear that the flight — the fact being established by verdict of the jury of the court of oyer and terminer — wrought an absolute forfeiture of all his personal estate.‡ This was the penalty for fleeing from justice, which was itself an offence, and the forfeiture incurred thereby was not to be remitted nor the forfeited goods restored, even if the defendant should be fully acquitted of the principal charge; nor could the verdict be reversed or set aside in any subsequent proceeding, except for error of law.

English seems to have been advised that some of the sheriff's doings were illegal; for he brought suit against him for seizing a cow and five swine, in August, 1692, laying his damage at fifteen pounds.§ In this action he was nonsuited, but upon what ground it does not appear; and thereupon he appealed to the Superior Court next to be held in Essex. Before this court sat, Corwin died, and the case seems to have proceeded no further, although, according to his own declara-

---

* I refer, for this and the subsequent proceedings of the Assembly upon applications for compensation, to the carefully collated extracts from the records, in the appendix to Mr. Moore's article.
† See his schedules of losses, and petition, in Mass. Archives, cxxxv. p. 127.
‡ 3 Inst., 232; Hawk. P. C., ii. chap. 9, §§ 27, 54; Black. Comm., iv. 387.
§ See Appendix G, and note § on the next page.

tion, he received sixty pounds from Corwin's administratrix.*
English in his application for compensation alleges that the
articles scheduled by him were "seized and taken away
chiefly by the sheriff and his under officers"; † but it is evident from the records of certain suits successfully prosecuted
by him against sundry of his neighbors, for helping themselves
to his property during his absence, that the officers of the law
were not the only trespassers upon the goods of the fugitive
merchant.‡

It would be interesting to learn why English, in his suit
against the sheriff, did not claim heavier damages, — whether
he was precluded by the certainty that the sheriff had a good
defence, in that his proceedings except in the small matter
sued for were strictly legal, or whether it was impossible to
prove the larger trespass by sufficient evidence, or whether
there was no prospect of recovering any considerable sum,
on account of the defendant's poverty.§ The pursuit of this
inquiry, however, even if there were any hope of a satisfactory result, must be deferred until the files of the Superior
Court are accessible.

It is certain that in the suit above mentioned English had
Corwin arrested and committed to jail on mesne process,‖
and that the entire personal estate of the latter which came
to the hands of his administratrix fell short of one hundred and
forty pounds.¶ Hence it may be reasonably inferred that the

---

* Note ¶ *infra*, Mass. Archives, cxxxv. p. 127.

† Mass. Archives, *ut supra*.

‡ English *v.* Pinsent, ex'x, and English *v.* Robinson, in I. C. C. P., Essex, March T. 1696, and also upon appeal in S. C. J.

§ It is said that English sued Corwin for £1500. Whether this report is from tradition, or from a wrong reading of the record of the case above described, is uncertain. No entry of such an action has been discovered.

It may be well here to explain another feature of this miserable business, which seems not to have been clearly understood. Mr. Upham has commented with severity (See Hist. Salem Witchcraft, vol. ii. p. 472) on the action of the Superior Court at the May term, 1694, at Ipswich, in granting Corwin a formal discharge from all liability for his official conduct; but this proceeding was in strict compliance with the requirement of the act of Nov. 17, 1693, "for passing sheriff's accompts" (1693-94, chap. 2: Province Laws, vol. i. p. 127), and was only a *quietus* the date of which, for the want of a general statute of limitations, the legislature had fixed as the beginning of a limited period within which suits against sheriffs should be brought, and was not intended as a bar to any action commenced within two years thereafter.

‖ See the constable's return, on the writ, Appendix G.

¶ Essex Probate files. Corwin's widow and administratrix twice prayed the judge of probate for an extension of time for rendering her account, alleging that there remained due £60 3s., which nearly corresponds with the sum that English admits he received from her. There is a tradition, which appears trustworthy, that, after his death, Corwin's relatives feared that English would literally "take the body" of the deceased, according to the precept of the court; and that therefore his remains were privately interred in the cellar of his dwelling-house, and reinterred, later, in his garden. The site of his tomb or grave can at this day be determined by record evidence.

sheriff had not enriched himself out of the spoil of his neighbors, — a conclusion which is confirmed by the finding of the court, upon the settlement of his official accounts, that there remained due to him, in 1693, a balance of £67 6s. 4d.*

Whether Corwin was a trespasser, or proceeded strictly according to law, it is clear that the province was equitably accountable to English for no more than it was pecuniarily benefited by his misfortune. If the sheriff's proceedings were unlawful, then he was solely and personally answerable. If his proceedings were legal, then only so much of the value of the forfeited goods as was realized upon their sale at public auction, according to law, enured to the public benefit; and it does not appear, and we certainly are not justified in assuming, that this exceeded or even equalled the £200 which were eventually ordered to be paid to him. Evidence is not wanting to the effect that there was great depreciation of value upon forced sales of the goods of the sufferers. The children of Giles Corey touchingly complain of having been obliged "to sell creatures and other things for a little more than half the worth of them," in order to get money to pay the sheriff, "and to maintain our father and mother in prison." †

But I proceed to another topic not discussed by Mr. Moore. As we have thus far scrutinized certain criticisms affecting the legality of some of the proceedings of the first Special Court of Oyer and Terminer of 1692, I may perhaps be excused for not omitting to consider another very grave, and now very important, statement impugning the validity of the court itself, repeatedly made, without contradiction, during the last forty or fifty years, by persons whose opinions are entitled to the highest respect.

Originally induced to doubt the legality of the court by Hutchinson's remark that, —

"By the charter, the general assembly are to constitute courts of justice, and the governor with the advice of council is to nominate and appoint judges, commissioners of oyer and terminer, &c.; but whether the governor, with advice of council, can constitute a court of oyer and terminer, without authority for that purpose derived from the general assembly, has been made a question,"

most recent writers upon the subject have outstripped him by declaring, unequivocally, that this court was illegal, because

---

* S. C. J., Essex, May T. 1694, and see note § on p. 19, *supra*.
† Mass. Archives, cxxxv. 161, and Hist. Coll. Essex Inst. i. p. 56.

it was not authorized by the Assembly.* I am constrained to
believe that these writers are wrong, and that the doubt
which Hutchinson records, but to which he is careful not
to lend the sanction of his own approval, is entirely unfounded.

The unanimity of these writers is not more remarkable
than the fact that the lawyers among them are the most
positive and emphatic in their expressions as to the invalidity of the commission under which the court was organized
and proceeded to judgment in those memorable trials. Thus,
Chandler declares that this court was, " beyond all question,
an illegal tribunal, because the governor had no shadow of
authority to constitute it;" and Washburn, that it " acted
without any valid authority, and perpetrated by its punishments a series of judicial murders without a parallel in
American History." And yet these confident and unqualified assertions are made notwithstanding the province charter
explicitly declares : —

" And Wee doe further Grant and Ordeyne that it shall and may
be lawfull for the said Governour with the advice and consent of the
Councill or Assistants from time to time to nominate and appoint
Judges Commissioners of Oyer and Terminer Sheriffs Provosts Marshalls Justices of the Peace and other Officers to our Councill and
Courts of Justice belonging."

On a casual reading of the charter no difficulty is perceived
in apprehending the meaning of this clause. There is no
inherent ambiguity and no necessary conflict with the subsequent clause which provides for the establishment of courts
of justice.†

The executive appointments authorized by this clause are

---

* Compare Hutchinson, Hist. Mass. Bay, 1st ed., ii. p. 48, with Bancroft, Hist.
U. S., 1st ed., iii. p. 88 [1840]; Washburn, Jud. Hist. Mass., 141 [1840] ; Quincy,
Hist. Harv. Univ., i. 179 [1840] ; Chandler, Criminal Trials, i. 92 [1844] ; Hildreth, Hist. U. S., ii. 156, 157 [1849–56]; Palfrey, Hist. N. E., iv. 105 [1875].
See also the more cautious statement of Upham, Hist. Salem Witchcraft, ii. 251,
252 [1867].

† " And wee doe of our further Grace certaine knowledge and meer moc̄on
Grant Establish and Ordaine for Vs our heires and Successors that the great
and Generall Court or Assembly of our said Province or Territory for the time
being Convened as aforesaid shall for ever have full Power and Authority to
Erect and Constitute Judicatories and Courts of Record or other Courts to be
held in the name of Vs Our heires and Successors for the Hearing Trying and
Determining of all manner of Crimes Offences Pleas Processes Plaints Acc̄ons
Matters Causes and things whatsoever ariseing or happening within Our said
Province or Territory or between persons Inhabiting or resideing there whether
the same be Criminall or Civill and whether the said Crimes be Capitall or not
Capitall and whether the said Pleas be Real personall or mixt and for the
awarding and makeing out of Execution thereupon."

those of, first, judges of the courts; second, commissioners of oyer and terminer; third, sheriffs; fourth, provosts; fifth, marshals; sixth, justices of the peace; seventh, other officers belonging to the council; eighth, other officers belonging to the courts of justice.

It is true that under this clause it belonged exclusively to the governor, by and with the advice and consent of the council, to appoint the judges and other officers of courts already erected by the legislature; but the issuing a commission of oyer and terminer by the executive alone, is not inconsistent with the full exercise of the functions of the general court, unless we assume that the issuing such a commission comprises the "erecting and constituting" of a court, within the meaning of the charter, which could only be done by the legislature.*

---

* In England the distinction between courts held under commissions of oyer and terminer, and the established courts at Westminster was fundamental, and well understood. Thus Fitzherbert says, "The writ of oyer and terminer should not properly be called a writ; but it is a commission directed unto certain persons when a great assembly, insurrection, or a heinous misdemeanor or trespass is committed and done in any place. In such case it is the manner and usage to make a commission of *oyer* and *terminer*, to hear and determine such misbehaviour," &c. (F. N. B., 110, B.) — and Hawkins, "It seems to be agreed, that where a statute prohibits a thing, and doth not appoint in what court it shall be punished, the offender may be indicted before justices of oyer and terminer, because the king hath a prerogative of suing in what court he will. But it hath been adjudged, that if such statute appoint that the offence shall be determined in the king's courts of record, it can be proceeded against only in one of the courts of Westminster Hall; because those being the highest courts of record, shall be intended to be only spoken of *secundum excellentiam*."— Pl. Crown, ii. 33.

The same distinction is observed, to-day, in the Dominion of Canada. There, notwithstanding the British North America Act, 1867, which is the organic law of the province, confers upon the governor-general the exclusive power of appointing the judges of the provincial courts — with certain express exceptions — the lieutenant-governors of New Brunswick and Ontario, in which provinces courts of oyer and terminer continue to be held, invariably issue the commissions for these courts; and what gives additional force to this as an instance in point is the fact that while the constitutionality of this practice has never been questioned, the authority of the governor-general in respect to the *personnel* of the established courts is so jealously maintained that his exclusive right to appoint queen's counsel, both in New Brunswick and Nova Scotia, in spite of an act in each of those provinces expressly conferring that power upon the governor of the province, has been judicially determined by the Supreme Court of Canada. Lenoir, *et al., v.* Ritchie, 3 Duval, 575.

In another aspect, the parallel between the present practice in New Brunswick, and that of the Province of Massachusetts Bay, in the issuing of commissions of oyer and terminer, is still closer; for, by clause 14 of section 92 of the British North America Act, "the administration of justice in the province, including the constitution, maintenance and organization of provincial courts both of civil and criminal jurisdiction," is wholly and exclusively devolved upon the provincial legislature, which has no power to delegate this authority, in any particular. It follows, therefore, that the issuing a commission of oyer and terminer by the lieutenant-governor is there clearly understood to be a proceeding essentially different from the act of constituting a criminal court, within the meaning of the act of parliament.

This assumption, it seems to me, is based upon a false theory. This theory not only implies that there is a conflict between two perfectly consistent clauses of the charter, but it cannot be maintained either as being sanctioned by the usage of this province, — which, beginning with the first administration under the charter, was invariably the opposite, — or by the authority of English law; and must not, therefore, be supposed to have been entertained by the framers of the charter, who were English lawyers, and undoubtedly meant to be understood here, as they would be understood in England.

It will be remembered that in England judges are appointed by the king, as the fountain of justice, in four ways; 1, by writ; 2, by patent; 3, by commission; and 4, by charter.* By the first method, the chief justice of the King's Bench,† and by the second, the ordinary judges of the established courts at Westminster are appointed; by the third, justices of oyer and terminer, jail delivery, assize and *nisi prius* receive their appointment; and by the fourth are constituted the judges in courts of corporations and inferior courts.

Under the last of these forms, namely, by charter, the courts of this province were indirectly brought into being; for the charter of the province is their ultimate foundation. By the third method, namely, by commission, courts of oyer and terminer were, immemorially, appointed in England; and this form of appointment, ratified by innumerable statutes and invariable practice, was as much a part of the law of England as any fundamental personal right that can be mentioned. Parliament had, from time to time, designated from what class the commissioners should be selected, but the right of nominating and appointing belonged solely to the king, or his chancellor—usually by commission, out of chancery, under the great seal. Now it is important to observe that the forms of the commissions or writs appointing commissioners of oyer and terminer were established by long usage, and could not be changed except by act of parliament. These forms declare the purpose of the commission, define the duties of the justices or commissioners, and fix the time and place for holding court, ‡ and the law required obedience from the people and

---

* Hale's Analysis of the Law, 19.
† See Life of Sir Matthew Hale, in preface to his Hist. of Eng. Law, xl.; and also Lord Mansfield's resignation of the chief-justiceship. — Annual Register for 1788, p. 241.
‡ The only form of a commission of oyer and terminer that has been discovered in the records of the province or of the provincial courts is that issued in 1698, for the trial of Jacob Smith. See Appendix H.

the proper local officers to all precepts legally issued and to
all rules and orders lawfully promulgated by the commissioners for the furtherance of their duties under these commissions. There was, therefore, in the issuing of a regular
commission of oyer and terminer, absolutely nothing for the
legislature to do, even if legislative interference were deemed
technically essential, except to declare that the exigency calling for the issuance of a commission had arisen; and even
this might be deemed an encroachment upon the prerogative.* When, however, it happened that new emergencies
arose for which the common law had made no adequate provision, the king was powerless to proceed without the aid of
parliament, and the latter in that case might, if it saw fit,
grant authority for the issuing of special commissions of oyer
and terminer, to be conducted under such regulations as the
parliament might prescribe, but still to be issued under the
royal seal, to contain all necessary and proper instructions
agreeable to law and be directed to such justices as the king
should appoint.†

Now this time-honored authority to issue commissions of
oyer and terminer is evidently what was intended by the king
to be delegated, in the charter, to his representative, the
governor, in the clause empowering him to nominate and
appoint commissioners of oyer and terminer.

Besides the general commissions of oyer and terminer
under which, together with the four other commissions, —
of the peace, jail-delivery, assize and *nisi prius*, — the king's
judges always conducted the business of their circuits (and
besides, a great number of other commissions to which further allusion is not necessary here), it was the immemorial
practice, sanctioned by many statutes ancient and modern,
to issue special commissions to hear and determine enormous crimes, where justice could not be effectually and
promptly administered through the ordinary tribunals, in
their regular sessions.‡ These, however, were to conform strictly to the ancient precedents, and could be superseded § if it should appear that the offences to be tried

---

* Hawk., P. C. ii., chaps. 1 and 5, §§ 1. Stat. 27 Hen. VIII., chap. 24.

† An instance of extraordinary special commission of this description was that issued under 19 Geo. II. c. 9, for the trial of the Scottish rebels in 1746, the proceedings of which were made the basis of Sir Michael Foster's Report and Discourses on Crown Law.

‡ 4 Inst. chap. xxviii.; Black. Comm. iv. 271.

§ The form of this supersedeas may be seen in the Register, pp. 124, 125, and Prynne, in his Animadversions on the Fourth part of Coke's Institute (p. 148), gives the record of another, *anno* 14 Ed. III.

under them were not sufficiently heinous; and the right of appointing the justices in these as well as other commissions belonged to the crown not only by a constitutional provision of the common law, but by solemn and express declaration of parliament.*

Nor was this power of appointment a menace to the liberties of the subject, since at these courts not only the attendance of grand and petit juries was secured, but it was an established principle that the king could not, without the aid of parliament, grant any new commission whatsoever that was not warranted by ancient precedent, however necessary it might seem; and, as all judges derived their authority from the crown, by some commission authorized by law, so they must exercise it in a legal manner.†

By the Statute of Westminster, the second (A.D. 1285),‡ while "the judges of either bench, and justices in eyre," were the only justices eligible to appointment upon general commissions of oyer and terminer, a wider range was allowed in the selection of special commissioners, on account of the supposed urgency of the cases in which their commissions were issued; and by subsequent statutes, justices of the peace, who, by their ordinary commissions had cognizance of felonies,§ were enabled to sit on these commissions "with others, the most worthy, of the county." ||

Such was the state of the English law at the time the province charter was granted, and these, it must be assumed, were the principles upon which corresponding tribunals were to be established in this province. In England, however, the king had authority to issue commissions of jail delivery, of assize, and of *nisi prius*, as well as those of justices of the peace ¶ and of oyer and terminer; but the governor's authority

---

* 27 Hen. VIII., chap. 24.

† Hawk., P. C. ii. chap. 1, §§ 8, 9. Moreover, courts of oyer and terminer were suspended or superseded whenever the justices of the King's Bench held assizes in the same county — Hale, P. C. 2, p. 4; Hawk., P. C. ii., chap. 5, § 3. As the Superior Court of Judicature of this province had all the authority of the court of King's Bench it would, unquestionably, have ousted the courts of oyer and terminer of all jurisdiction whenever it should happen that the two tribunals sat simultaneously in the same county.

‡ 13 Ed. I., chap. 29.

§ Lamb. Eirenarcha (ed. 1610), 553.

|| 42 Ed. III., chap. 4.

¶ Justices of the peace were judges of record, and held courts of common-law jurisdiction in the establishment of which it cannot be supposed and will not be claimed that any legislative action was necessary. The exclusive right of the governor and council to appoint these justices is clear and unquestionable, and if the clause in the charter conferring authority upon the legislature to erect judicatories and courts of record is to have the interpretation contended for by

to issue commissions was, by the charter, limited to the two classes last named. Hence, whenever, in this province, it became necessary to appoint commissioners of oyer and terminer, with extraordinary powers, — for instance, to clear the jails, or to try an indictment found by another tribunal, or to hear and determine offences not cognizable by them at the common law, — the legislature supplied the executive disability by an enabling act; and instances of this kind will be presently considered.

Of course this discussion is strictly confined to the common-law tribunals, and therefore what I have said about the limit of executive authority under the charter does not apply to those courts which derived their functions from the civil law; for it will not be contended that either our probate courts, which rest upon no other foundation than a delegation of authority from the governor, as the supreme ordinary, without any enabling act of the legislature, or the courts of admiralty, the establishment of which was, in the charter, specially reserved to the crown, were illegally constituted, and their proceedings void.

On referring to the judicial records, as far back even as the time of Andros, we find that courts of oyer and terminer, after the English models, were held in Massachusetts for the trial of felonies, as a matter of course;* and, after the establishment of government under the charter, that there were no less than fourteen such courts,† of which eight were constituted by the governor's commission as special courts, in accordance with the ordinary English precedents, and without any authority from the legislature. Two of these eight commissions were issued in 1692, and the last in 1713.

Of the remaining six courts of oyer and terminer held during the provincial period, two were held by virtue of the

---

those who claim that it deprives the executive of all power to constitute in any manner a judicial tribunal capable of action, it follows that in this province, commissions of justices of the peace were, of themselves, of no more force than blank parchment. Such a construction nullifies the authority clearly intended to be conferred upon the executive by the charter, and involves the absurdity of granting a power and at the same time defeating the exercise of it; for justices of the peace, by virtue of their commissions alone, were not merely conservators of the peace, but magistrates whose judicial functions, inseparable from their office, were various, important, and well defined by the common law. The legislature might have enlarged or diminished their jurisdiction, or, perhaps, have transferred the whole of it to another tribunal; but, until such legislative action, it cannot be imagined how they could legitimately have borne the title and yet not have had the authority which went with it.

* Superior Court records.
† Appendix I.

act of 1696 against piracy and robbing upon the sea;* which, being for the punishment of offences not cognizable at the common law, and therefore not comprehended in any established form of commission, required the sanction of the legislature. Of the rest of these six commissions, the first† was issued for the trial of an offender already imprisoned upon an indictment returnable before the Superior Court, and whose case, therefore, could not come under the jurisdiction of a court constituted by the ordinary commission, which conferred no authority to demand from the clerk of another tribunal, the indictment in his custody. In this case, also, as well as in the three cases that remain to be considered, the alleged offenders had been duly committed to jail, and therefore it became necessary for the legislature to enlarge the power of the commissioners so as to enable them to bring these offenders before them. It is noticeable that while the preamble of each of these acts recites that the case ought, "as the law stands, to be tried by a special court of assize," they agree in expressly declaring that "a court of oyer and terminer have and can exercise the same jurisdiction and authority in all capital offences."

An examination of all the legislation respecting courts of oyer and terminer throughout the provincial period, shows that there was never an attempt by the assembly to formally establish such a tribunal. The acts amounted only to an authorization, or, at most, to a *fiat*, that commissions should issue; but the form of the commission and the particular directions to the justices were left to the governor in each case, in accordance with, or in analogy to, the usual common-law precedents. Indeed, any legislative act establishing a special court of oyer and terminer according to the common law would amount to no more than a mere *fiat*, since the commission to the justices must, necessarily, conform to established precedents. Such an act would not only be

---

* Province Laws, 1696, chap. 4. This was, substantially, a re-enactment of the act of parliament 27 Hen. VIII., chap. 4, which allowed offences previously exclusively cognizable by the courts of admiralty to be tried by commissioners of oyer and terminer and a jury. If the act of parliament extended to this province, the offender, to get the benefit of it, must needs be carried to England for trial in some shire of the realm. The province law gave him the same privilege here. The counsel for Ansel Nickerson, who was tried for his life before a court of admiralty in Boston in 1769, claimed the right to be tried by a jury; but from the confused and incomplete accounts of that trial, it is impossible to determine whether the right was claimed under this act or upon other grounds. John Adams had "half a mind to undertake" the publication of the record of that case. It is to be regretted that his "mind" was thus divided. — See his Diary, Dec. 23, 1769.

† Province Laws, 1718–19, chap. 19.

superfluous, but irregular, because the power intended to be
conferred thereby had already been, more authoritatively, and
quite as clearly, given by 'the charter ; and the legislature
would transcend its proper functions in attempting either to
reinforce or detract from the fundamental law.*

The issuing of commissions of oyer and terminer having
been found inexpedient, — less, probably, on account of difficulty in securing proper persons off the bench of the Superior
Court than on account of the want of system in conducting
the proceedings and preserving the records of these extraordinary courts, the extra expense which they occasioned, and
the perplexities involved in harmonizing their operations with
those of the regular judicatories established by statute, —
and, nevertheless, it being evident that some means should
be provided for bringing offenders to justice in the long vaca-
tions of the Superior Court,† — the legislature, in 1713,
passed the "Act for holding Special Courts of Assize and
General Goal Delivery." ‡

By this act it was made lawful for the governor, by and
with the advice and consent of the council, upon any such
extraordinary occasion or emergency as would justify the
appointing of a commission of oyer and terminer, to issue " a
precept directed to the justices of the court of assize and
general goal delivery," requiring them to hold a special court
of assize and general jail delivery.

Although after the passage of this act no commission of
oyer and terminer seems to have been issued without the
concurrence of the General Court, it is by no means certain that this act suspended or superseded the authority
conferred on the governor by the charter. This act was
so loosely drawn that when a special session under it was
ordered to be held at York, Feb. 22, 1749,§ the only two
justices who were able to reach the place at the appointed
time found not only that they had no authority to adjourn
the court until a quorum should arrive, but that the act
had given to the court thus appointed a new name, by
which, it might be claimed, a new tribunal had been established independent of the Superior Court; in which case its
organization was imperfect in some essential particulars. The

---

* See observations of the Privy Council on the provincial act of 1692–93,
chap. 9. — Province Laws, i. p. 37, note.

† In some counties, the sessions of the Superior Court were, for years,
entirely discontinued ; and the stated terms in most counties were held but once
or twice a year.

‡ 1713–14, chap. 5.

§ Mass. Archives, vols. xxxi. p. 690, and xxxii. p. 1.

case for which this court was appointed was afterwards tried at a stated term of the Superior Court in the same county,* and the law was amended by the passage of the later " Act for holding a Superior Court of Judicature, Court of Assize and General Goal Delivery at other times than those already appointed by law." †

I conclude my reference to the provincial statutes upon this subject by adding that the court of oyer and terminer authorized to be appointed by the " Act against Jesuits and Popish Priests" ‡ affords only additional proof of what I have herein maintained. The offence denounced by that act was created by it, and was therefore cognizable by commissioners of oyer and terminer, by virtue of this statute only, and not at common law. Here, moreover, it appears that the authority to issue the commission was again given in general terms, and the details were left to the executive to arrange, in analogy to the regular precedents. And I will add, further, that, at the time of the enactment of the statute for passing of sheriffs' accounts, to which I have referred in another connection,§ and which was a standing law of the province for regulating the estreats of all fines, &c., in any " special court of oyer and terminer," &c., only two such courts had been appointed — one of which was the tribunal for trying the persons accused of witchcraft — and that the commissions, in both instances, were issued by the governor, by and with the advice and consent of the council, and without the concurrence of the legislature.

Upon the familiar facts which I have thus minutely reviewed, and for the reasons I have given, I think it must be conceded that the authority of Phips to appoint the commission, in 1692, which has such a deplorable record, is fully vindicated by the express language of the charter, by the invariable practice of the executive department of the province, and by the constant connivance of the legislature, — which, in an act that continued in force as late as 1775,‖ established the secretary's fee for writing and sealing such commissions at 6s. 8d. each. The court thus constituted had, by the common law, all necessary power to issue *venires* for grand and petit jurors — to be drawn and returned according to the colonial laws then in force ; to proceed to inquire, hear and determine, according to the precept of the commission ; to

---

* The King *v.* Obadiah Albee, York, June T. 1750. Benjamin Le Dite was tried in the same county, as accessory, June, 1751. — Records of S. C. J., 1750-51, fols. 31 and 237.
† Province Laws, 1750-51, chap. 13. ‡ *Ibid.*, 1700-1701, chap. 1.
§ See note § p. 19, *ante*. ‖ Province Laws, 1772-73, chap. 42.

compel the attendance of witnesses, and to administer the necessary oaths to them and to the jurors and officers of the court; to take testimony; to ascertain and decree forfeitures and to impose fines and amercements; and, finally, to pass sentence of death.

There remain, therefore, for consideration only two questions: first, were the persons appointed, legally eligible? and, second, did the exigency, according to established rules, justify the issuing of a special commission?

Happily we are freed from all doubt as to the qualifications of the judges. By an inspection of the records of the executive council, it appears that they were all members of that board, and that besides the evidence of superior fitness manifest in their holding this high position, to which they were called by royal favor, the name of each of them had, previous to their appointment upon this tribunal, been ordered to be inserted in all commissions of the peace, as a justice of the peace and of the quorum in his own county.*

As to the urgency of the occasion which, it was claimed, demanded this exercise of executive authority, I submit that charity and common sense alike require that the action of the governor and his advisers should be judged by contemporary standards, and not according to the high scale of modern science, and the fine humanity of modern dealings with crime; and, further, that an error of discretion, however gross, if the mistaken action did not transcend the limits of the agent's authority, cannot invalidate the act.

The determining of the existence of the emergency for a special commission of oyer and terminer, it must be admitted, was the exclusive province of the executive at that time, and not ours of to-day; and, assuming that the act was done in good faith, the actors are not amenable to posterity for any fault more censurable than an error of judgment. But did they err in judgment? I think not. Our fathers believed the Sacred Scriptures, literally; and the human statutes against witchcraft were, according to their belief, specially and peculiarly reinforced by the divine command, "Thou shalt not suffer a witch to live." All the old lawyers had placed this "horrible and detestable" crime next after treason, and at the head of the list of felonies. Here, in 1692, the clamor against alleged witches, which even the reverend clergy were active in fomenting, was loud and pervading. The jails were overflowing with the accused, and with the

---

* Vol. ii. p. 175.

witnesses against them,—some of whom had been incarcerated for months,— and new members of the diabolical confederacy were daily being discovered.

The charter did not require that a general court should be held the first year,* and, until it was convened, there could be no establishment of regular judicatories. No adequate provision was made by law for reimbursing the marshals and jail-keepers their expenses in supporting poor prisoners in their custody; and the charge of maintaining those who belonged to families not indigent was ruinous to their estates, and burdensome in the extreme to their friends and relatives who were called upon to visit them in prison—often remote from their homes — and to advance the means of ministering to their wants. It was not likely that any legislative provision would be made before the approach of winter, and it seemed probable that no place of confinement could be found sufficient to contain the multitude that would be held for trial by that time.† The offence being fully recognized by the law, and the charges legally and formally made, with what fairness can it be averred that under such circumstances the appointing of a special commission, to release the prisoners, by acquittal or conviction, was hasty and ill-advised ? Speaking from the standpoint of 1692, I think I am not rash in venturing the opinion that the authorities were more properly chargeable with hesitancy and delay than with precipitation; and that if, between the date of the charter and the assembling of the general court, there was no law against felony, and no possible tribunal for redressing public wrongs, the good people of this comparatively enlightened province were in a condition of anarchy as unfortunate as the assertion of its ever having existed is preposterous. Such a state of affairs is inconceivable in any community of Englishmen outside of bedlam.

I think it will be difficult, upon the most minute and thorough examination of this subject, to discover that I have omitted any fact that may furnish sufficient grounds for the doubt which Hutchinson started. I say started, for it is remarkable that neither Oldmixon, Douglass, Neal, Burke,

---

* Hutchinson's Hist. Mass. Bay, 1st ed., ii. pp. 14, 15.

† "May 27 [June 6, N. S.], 1692. Upon consideration that there are many Criminal Offenders now in Custody, some whereof have lyen long & many inconveniences attending the thronging of the Goals at this hot season of the year ; there being no Judicatories or Courts of Justice yet Established." — Preamble to the order for the Court of Oyer and Terminer : Executive Records of the Council, vol. ii. p. 176.

nor Chalmers gives any hint that the special court at Salem was irregular, — and Chalmers, certainly, if the court had not been legally constituted, would not have failed to animadvert upon the gross blunder of Phips and his advisers.

I trust I do not offend when I say, what I hope to be able to show conclusively on some other occasion, that Hutchinson, who was not altogether free from the imperfection to which the most careful are liable, of sometimes misrepresenting facts, was, also, astute in the discovery of legal novelties that will not stand the test of critical examination. Though not regularly bred to the law, his reading of legal authorities was extensive and critical, but his perceptions were, if sharp, too narrow. He misstated the laws of the colony, both in his history and as a public officer, when he had no excuse for error; and, towards the end of his official career, while he was steadfast in his intention to support the prerogative at all hazards, he was, in his disputes with the popular party, and in the opinions which he officially expressed, oftener wrong than right on matters of law. If he really entertained the doubt which, from the importance it derives through his mention of it, has been fostered and strengthened until it has ripened into assurance, he was evidently mistaken. It is more likely, however, that the passage in his history, upon which a modern judgment has been founded disparaging the able men to whose management the government of the province was, at first, confided, was prompted by his recollection of some of those subtile criticisms to which the clauses in the charter relating to the establishment of courts and the appointment of judges were subjected, in the disputes that were renewed upon the choice of a successor to Attorney-General Overing, during the period with which the second volume of his history closes. That controversy was carried on with great zeal and acuteness, not to say acrimony, and doubtless left a lasting impression.*

The supersedure of the Special Court of Oyer and Terminer by the establishment of the Superior Court of Judicature,† has sometimes been so mentioned as to convey the impression that it was an intentional rebuke of the manner

---

* There can be little doubt that the views which Pownall expressed in his "Administration of the Colonies" (p. 72, *et seq.*) were imbibed through his interest in these discussions. He says (p. 75) that it is "a maxim universally maintained by the colonists, that no court can be erected but by act of legislature"; but the context clearly shows that the courts here intended are fixed and established judicatories, and that he had no reference to commissions of oyer and terminer.

† Province Laws, 1692-93, chap. 33.

in which the earlier tribunal was constituted and had conducted its proceedings. Nothing can be more gratuitous than such an insinuation. There never was any express dissolution of the Court of Oyer and Terminer. As has been already shown, its functions ceased, *ipso facto*, the moment a competent court of assize and jail delivery began its sessions within the same jurisdiction.* That such a court would be held in Essex County was foreseen when the act establishing the Superior Court was passed at the session of the Assembly which began on the 12th of October; and an extraordinary term of assize and jail delivery was specially appointed by the legislature, during the same session,† for the purpose of trying fresh indictments for witchcraft. This court, so far from being essentially a new tribunal, was held, with a single exception, by judges, with Stoughton still at their head, who had sat in the former trials.

The new court of assize recommenced the work of prosecuting witches with increased vigor. The new grand juries, obedient to the charges of the court, found fresh bills of indictment for witchcraft; and it is said that not less than fifty-six of these were preferred at the first term. Certain it is that, at the special term at Salem, at the first regular term for Middlesex, in the same month, and at the term held at Ipswich, in the following month, thirty-one indictments against persons accused of covenanting with the devil or practising acts of witchcraft were tried, and that in all but three of these cases the petit juries found verdicts of "not guilty." Those who were not acquitted were afterwards reprieved or pardoned.

It would seem, therefore, after all, that we are more indebted to the practical common-sense of that most popular tribunal, *the jury*, than to all other influences, for putting a stop to those scenes of horror which all the rules of evidence, as then understood and practised in the most enlightened courts, all the skill and acumen of a trained attorney for the prosecution, and all the wisdom of a grave, learned, and pious bench of judges were powerless to prevent.

It is an important fact, but one which seems to have been overlooked by all writers upon these witch-trials, that in the

---

* See note † on page 25, *ante*.
† *Ibid.*, chap. 45. From Sewall's Diary, under date of Oct. 26, 1692, it appears " that the Court of Oyer and Terminer " counted " themselves dismissed " by the vote on a bill for " a Fast and Convocation of Ministers, that [we] may be led in the right way as to the Witchcrafts." This was a measure promoted by the friends and relatives of the accused. Three days later, according to the same authority, Governor Phips decided that the court "must fall."

later cases of witchcraft the jurors were chosen by, and from among, all those inhabitants of the province who possessed the requisite amount of property to qualify them as electors under the new charter. The act requiring this qualification for jurors was passed Nov. 25, 1692;* and though an earlier act had prescribed the same qualification for jurors serving at the courts of general sessions and of common pleas,† no such rule had been made or adopted for the Special Court of Oyer and Terminer. The only *venire* for this last-named court, that has been preserved,‡ was for the September term, and is directed to the sheriff, requiring him to impanel and return, as petit jurors, "good and lawful men of the *freeholders and other freemen*" of his bailiwick. Thus it seems that before the assizes were established, the jurors were chosen, as in colonial times, from among the *freemen* only; and these being, by the old law, necessarily church-members, were more likely to implicitly obey the directions of the judges,—with whose prejudices they were in full sympathy,—than were those selected in each town by the whole body of electors, which had been enlarged and liberalized, in conformity with the requirements of the charter, by the inclusion of a considerable proportion of respectable persons not members of the orthodox communion. That the influence of this new element in the body politic was felt in the matter of selecting jurors for the Superior Court, appears, to some extent, in the rejection of numerous indictments laid before the grand juries, though not in so marked a degree as in the large proportion of verdicts of acquittal.

I close with some reflections suggested by the solemn tragedy of 1692, and the comments and censures of those who have written upon this instructive passage in our annals. I cannot conceive why men should ever willingly misrepresent, suppress, or forget any of the incidents of an event so important. History, if it is, as is said, philosophy teaching by examples, needs to have its practical expositions freed from all error, and clear as noonday even to their remotest and minutest details. Otherwise the lesson may be profitless; for the slightest departure from truth in one particular may open wide an inevitable channel of error. And it is neither philosophical nor profitable, it seems to me, to be sedulously searching for some individual or class upon whom to fasten the responsibility for the errors and wrong-doings of a whole

---

* Province Laws, 1692–93, chap. 33.   † *Ibid.*, chap. 9.
‡ Woodward, vol. i. p. 10.

people. Lawyers and laymen, as well as clergymen, were equally under the influence of the superstitious terrors of that day of darkness and delusion. This common responsibility of all classes of the community is not, however, to be equally apportioned; for the educated men who directed the public mind, controlled public affairs, established the courts, and administered the laws, made, by accepting their high posts, a virtual profession of superior qualifications for instructing and governing, and they are, therefore, justly held to stricter accountability and to a larger share of blame. There were, indeed, a few that were not deluded; but those who were thus happily distinguished from the mass were not confined to any particular rank or calling.

Besides the important aid which the details of this sad story afford in the investigation of those obscure laws of psychology which science is just beginning to understand, the chief lesson that the story teaches, as I apprehend, is not that one class of society is less to be trusted than another, but that superstition should neither be sanctioned by the law, nor permitted by legal authority to take the least aggressive action against any individual. This experience of our fathers teaches us that the legitimate province of government is full large when confined to the practical affairs of real life, and that the functions of the magistracy can never be properly directed against evils which only affect the moral and spiritual welfare of individuals, or which are purely imaginary and subjective.

The tragedy of 1692 was the last exhibition of the kind possible in Massachusetts; and in this we were happier than most, if not all, other Christian communities. Out of that dark and terrible ordeal we emerged into a new existence. From the year 1692 dates the rise of a healthy scepticism on the subject of demonology, and the decline of the prestige of the clergy who habitually denounced those that dared to doubt its reality. Thenceforth men began to indulge less exclusively in the contemplation of the supernatural, and to turn their attention more and more to the practical affairs of life. Yet such was the persistency of the ideas which had dominated the human mind for centuries, that, whatever speculations of incredulity even the educated classes may have favorably entertained in private, few dared openly to express their utter disbelief in demonology for more than a century later. Our charity for the mistakes of our ancestors should be greatly increased by the reflection that though, fortunately, our statute books and court records have not been blemished by acts of persecution touching the recent endemic of spiritualism, we of this generation have, in the spread of that infatuation, had ample opportunity to see repeated, and to observe the contagion of, the "phenomena" of witchcraft, dissociated from diabolism and so disguised as to fascinate and convince minds which we had supposed were unsusceptible of such irrational influences, and proof against deception.

APPENDIX.

A.

The first council summoned by Andros ordered proclamation to be made continuing all civil officers, and declaring that "the laws not repugnant to the laws of England in the several colonies should be observed during His Excellency's pleasure." This appears in a fragment of the original record still remaining in the secretary's office (also printed in Mass. Hist. Coll. 2d series, vol. viii.) although in the copy which was transcribed for the Commonwealth from the state papers of England the clause relating to continuing the laws is omitted. By a subsequent proclamation (Mar. 8, 1686-7), all laws "not repugnant to the laws of England, his majesty's commission for government, and indulgence in matters of religion, nor any law or order not already passed by the governor and council," were confirmed and continued. Under Dudley, former civil officers were temporarily continued in their places, the laws were revised, as if of force, and the judgments of the colonial courts affirmed, on *scire facias*, in the newly appointed tribunals. — Compare executive records of the council, vol. ii. pp. 23, 34, 51, *et seq.*, with Mass. Archives, cxxvi. pp. 272, 273.

The statute of 1 James I., chap. 12, was enacted before the settlement of the Massachusetts Bay, and, according to the rule that English emigrants carry the law with them, it would have been effectual here, if it had not been superseded by the colonial ordinance upon the same subject, which was borrowed from the Mosaic law. Newton, who was appointed at the organization of the court of Oyer and Terminer to act as prosecuting attorney, seems to have followed the English precedents of indictments under the act of James; and the allegations in the indictments drawn by him conclude "against the form of the statute," &c. In only two instances, however, does he expressly mention the statute of James, as is done in the English precedents; these are the second indictments against Rebecca Eames and Samuel Wardwell, respectively, which appear to have been drawn in blank by him, and afterwards filled in by Checkley. They are for covenanting with the devil, and are printed in Woodward, vol. i. pp. 143 and 147. Checkley — who was chosen attorney-general June 14, 1689, although he did not succeed Newton in the prosecution of the alleged witches until July 26, 1692 — seems, in the indictments which he himself drew, to have treated the offence as a violation of the colony law; and his indictments conclude, "against the laws in that case made and provided."— See Mass. Archives, cxxxv. p. 101, and elsewhere.

It is hard to form a satisfactory conjecture as to the cause of the confusion in the forms of indictments preferred at different times during the course of these prosecutions. It is not improbable that the violation of different statutes may have been purposely charged on account of the very uncertainty of the law, and, where different indictments were found against the same person, from a desire to hold the prisoner to answer to at least one valid indictment. On the other hand, there is no indication of any doubt or scruple in the minds of the judges, who, in that period of loose criminal practice, were probably not more solicitous for the safety of culprits than were contemporary judges in England, and who doubtless were entirely satisfied with the very general advice of the reverend clergy, in their "Return," to them and their associates in the council: "Nevertheless, we cannot but humbly recommend unto the government the speedy and vigorous prosecutions of such as have rendered themselves obnoxious, according to the directions given in the laws of God, and the wholesome statutes of the English nation, for the detection of witchcrafts." — Hutchinson's Hist. vol. ii. p. 51.

Lambard, evidently, did not deem it important to furnish any form of indictment for a capital offence under the act of James, except where the practice of diabolical acts had caused death; the offence described in the only other precedent given by him — that for bewitching a horse — not being capital. 3 Inst. 46. None of the indictments before the Special Court of Oyer and Terminer contain the allegation of killing by witchcraft, and yet all were tried as capital offences, which, however, they would have been, according to the form of the allegations, either under the English statute, or the law of the colony.

B.

(*Power of attorney to Stephen Sewall.*)

Whereas we the Subscribers are Informed that His Excellency the Governour: Honourable Council, and Generall assembly of this Province have been pleased to hear Our Supplication and answer our Prayer in passing an act in favour of us respecting our Reputations and Estates; Which we humbly and gratefully acknowledge.

And inasmuch as it would be Chargeable and Troublesome for all or many of us to goe to Boston on this affair:— Wherefore we have and do Authorize, and Request our Trusty Freind the Worshipfull Stephen Sewall Esqr:

To procure us a Coppy of the said act, and to doe what may be further proper and necessary for the reception of what is allowed us and to take and receive the same for us and to Transact any other Thing referring to the Premises on our Behalf that may be requisite or Convenient. —

Essex December 1711

John Eames in behalf of
  his mother Rebecca Eames
Abigail Faulkner
Samuel Preston on behalf
  of his wife Sarah Preston.
Samuel Osgood on behalf
  of his mother Mary Osgood
Nathaniel Dane
Joseph Wilson
Samuel Wardwell
John Wright
Ebenezer Barker
Francis Johnson on behalf
  of his mother, Brother &
  Sister Elizabeth.
Joseph Emerson on behalf
  of his wife martha Emerson
  of Haverhill
Ephraim Willdes

Charles Burrough — eldest [son]
John Barker
Lawrence Lacy
Abraham Foster
John Parker   } y[e] sons of
Joseph Parker } Mary Parker
                 } deceased
John Marston
Thomas Carrier
John Frie
Mary Post
John[:] Johnson in behalf of his
  mother Rebecca Johnson & his
  sister
William Barker sen[r]
Gorge Jacob on behalf of
  his father who suffer[d]
Thorndik Procter on behalf
  of his Father. John Procter
  who suffered
                      aboues[d]
Beniamin Procter son of the
John Moulton on behalf of his wife
Elizabeth the daughter: of Giles Coree
  who suferd
Robert Pease on behalf of his wife
Annies King on behalf of heir mother
Doarcas hoare
Willem town
Samuel nurs
Jacob Estei
Edward Bishop. — *Witchcraft Papers in Clerk's Office, Essex*, vol. ii. 64.

C.

(Letter of Nehemiah Jewett to Stephen Sewall, with list of claims.)

Mr SEWALL & Hon^rd freind

Sr Respects p̄mised yo^rs I receiued p̄ yor Son bearing date ye 27th of this Instant moth & according to yor desire I haue drawne out ye names & Sums (of ye Respectiue Sufferers) y^t ye petitione^rs prayd for.

1st of those executed

Elizabeth How; Mary & Abigail her daughters prayd for	12 . 0 . 0
Georg Jacobs. Georg Jacobs his son prayd ⅌ :	79 . 0 . 0
Sarah Wild. Ephraim Wild her son prayd for	14 . 0 . 0
Mary Easty. Isaack Easty her husband pr^d ⅌	20 . 0 . 0
Mary Parker Joseph & Jno. Parker her Sons pr^d ⅌	08 . 0 . 0
Mr Georg Burroughs. Charles Burroughs his son pr^d ⅌	50 . 0 . 0
Elizabeth Core. & Martha ye wife of Jno. Molton he pr^d ⅌	21 . 0 . 0
Rebecca Nurse. Samuell Nurse her Son pr^d ⅌	25 . 0 . 0
Jno. Willard. Majeret Towne his relict pr^d ⅌	20 . 0 . 0
Sarah Good. William Good her husband pr^d ⅌	30 . 0 . 0
Martha Carried Thomas Carriar her husband pr^d ⅌	07 . 6 . 0
Samuell Wardell. Executed & his wife Sarah Condemn^d	
Samuell Wardell their Son. pr^d ⅌	36 .15 . 0
John Procter. Jno. & Thorndick his sons pr^d ⅌	150 . 0 . 0

p̄sons Condemned & not Executed

Mrs Mary Bradbury Henry & Saml True her sons pr^d ⅌	020 . 0 . 0
Abgail Faulkner for her & her children pr^d ⅌	020 .0 . 0
Anigail Hobs. William Hobs her Father pr^d ⅌ 10^{li}	010 . 0 . 0
Aen Foster. Abraham Foster her son pr^d ⅌	006 .10 . 0
Robeccah Eames. prayes ⅌	010 . 0 . 0
Drcas King alius whore pr^d ⅌	021 .13 . 0
Mary Post prayes ⅌.	008 .14 . 0
Mary Lacy. Lawrence her husband pr^d ⅌	0:08 .10 . 0
Elizabeth Procter & ⎫ I find their names amongst ye aboue	
Elizabeth Johnson ⎭ condemned p̄sons & no sum put to them	

p̄sons Imprison^d, & not Condemned petitioned for Allowances for their Imprisonm^t charges &^c.

Sarah Buckley & Mary Witredg for so much they pay^d	15 - 0 - 0
John Johnson for Rebecca his wife & daughter	6 - 0 - 4
Capt Osgoods wife Mary	5 - 7 - 4
Sarah Cole for hers	6 -10 - 0
Edward Bishop petitions for	100 - 0 - 0

Jn̊ Barker ℔ Marya Barker his daughters expences he
p^d for her. . . . . 03 -15 -10
Rob Pease ℔ his . . . . 13 - 3 - 0
Nathl Dane — ℔ his . . . . 4 -13 - 0
Jn̊ Fry ℔ his . . . . 4 -17 - 4
Joseph Wilson ℔ his . . . . 4 -15 - 4
Jn̊ Wright — ℔ his . . . . 0 - 4 - 0
Mercy Woodell ye wife of Jn̊ Wright for hers . . . . 5 - 4 - 0
Jn̊ Barker prayes for his Br̊ Wm Barkers . . . . . 3 -11 - 0
Lawrenc Lasy for his daughter Mary . . . . 3 - 0 - 4
Jn̊ Marston ℔ his wife . . . . 2 -14 - 0
Ebenezer Barker for his wife . . . . 5 - 7 - 4
Francis Johnson for his wife then Sarah Hawks . . . 5 - 4 - 0
Francis Johnson for his mother . . . . 7 -12 - 0
& for his Sister Elizabeth . . . . 3 -00 - 0

Ips. 28. 9- 1711.   Totall 796 -18 - 0

besides Mr English his demaunds Left to ye Courts Consideration & determination.

   S^r y^{or} Most humble servant.

            NEH: JEWET — *Ibid.*, 67.

D.

(Report of the committee on claims of sufferers.)

Oct. 26, 1711. . . . Report of the Committee appointed, Relating to the Affair of Witchcraft in the Year 1692, Viz,

We whose Names are subscribed in Obedience to your Honours Act at a Court held the last of May 1710, for our inserting the Names of the several Persons who were condemned for Witchcraft in the year 1692, & of the Damages they sustained by their Prosecution; Being met at Salem, for the Ends aforesaid the 13th Septem^r 1710, Upon Examination of the Records of the several Persons condemned, Humbly offer to your Honours the Names as follows, to be inserted for the Reversing their Attainders ; — Elizabeth How, George Jacob, Mary Easty, Mary Parker, Mr George Burroughs, Gyles Cory & Wife, Rebecca Nurse, John Willard, Sarah Good, Martha Carrier, Samuel Wardel, John Procter, Sarah Wild, Mary Bradbury Abigail Falkner Abigail Hobbs Ann Foster, Rebecca Eams, Dorcas Hoar, Mary Post, Mary Lacy:

And having heard the several Demands of the Damages of the aforesaid Persons & those in their behalf ; & upon Conference have so moderated their respective Demands, that We doubt not but they will be readily complied with by your Honours.

Which respective Demands are as follows

Elizabeth How, Twelve Pounds; George Jacob, Seventy nine Pounds; Mary Easty, Twenty Pounds; Mary Parker, Eight Pounds, Mr George Burroughs, Fifty Pounds, Gyles Core & Martha Core his Wife, Twenty one Pounds; Rebecca Nurse Twenty five Pounds, John Willard, Twenty Pounds, Sarah Good, Thirty Pounds Martha Carrier, Seven Pounds six shillings, Samuel Wardell & Sarah his Wife, Thirty six Pounds fifteen shillings; John Proctor & . . . Proctor his Wife, One hundred & fifty Pounds, Sarah Wilde, Fourteen Pounds; Mrs Mary Bradbury, Twenty Pounds; Abigail Faulkner, Twenty Pounds; Abigail Hobbs, Ten Pounds; Ann Foster, Six Pounds ten shillings; Rebecca Eams, Ten Pounds; Dorcas Hoar, Twenty one Pounds seventeen shillings; Mary Post Eight Pounds fourteen shillings; Mary Lacey Eight Pounds ten shillings: — The Whole amounting unto Five Hundred & seventy eight Pounds, & twelve shillings. —

(Sign'd)

J.^{no} APPLETON THOMAS NOYES JOHN BURRILL NEHEM.^{h} JEWETT. SALEM, Septem.^{r} 14. 1711.

Read & Accepted in the House of Represent.^{ves} Signed John Burrill Speak.^{r}

Read & Concur'd in Council; —— Consented to J DUDLEY.

—*Council Records*, vol. ix. p. 134.

E.

(*Copy of the warrant for payment of claims.*)

By His Excellency the Gouerno.^{r}

Whereas ye Generall Assembly in their last Session accepted ye report of their comitte appointed to consider of ye Damages Sustained by Sundry persons prosecuted for Witchcraft in ye year 1692 Viz.^{t}.

	£ s. d.		£ s. d.
To Elizabeth How	12 - 0 -0	John Procter & wife	150 - 0 -0
George Jacobs	79 - 0 -0	Sarah Wild	014 - 0 -0
Mary Eastey	20 - 0 -0	Mary Bradbury	20 - 0 -0
Mary Parker	08 - 0 -0	Abigail Faulkner	20 - 0 -0
George Burroughs	50 - 0 -0	Abigail Hobbs	10 - 0 -0
Giles corey & wife	21 - 0 -0	Anne Foster	6 -10 -0
Rebeccah Nurse	25 - 0 -0	Rebeccah Eames	10 - 0 -0
John Willard	20 - 0 -0	Dorcas Hoar	21 -17 -0
Sarah Good	30 - 0 -0	Mary Post	8 -14 -0
Martha Currier	7 - 6 -0	Mary Lacey	8 -10 -0
Samuel Wardwell & wife	36 -15 -0		
	———		269 -11 -00
	309 -01 -00		309 - 1 -00
			578 -12 -00

The whole amounting vnto Five hundred Seventy Eight poundes & Twelue Shillings.

I doe by & with the advice & consent of Her Maj^{teys} council hereby order you to pay ye aboue Sum of fiue hundred Seuenty Eight poundes & Twelue shillings to Stephen Sewall Esqr. who together with ye Gentlemen of ye Comitte that Estimated and Reported ye Said Damages are desired & directed to distribute ye Same in proportion as aboue to Such of ye Said persons as are Liuing & to those that legaly represent them that are dead according as ye law directs for which this Shall be your Warrant —

Giuen vnder my hand at Boston
the 17 day of December 1711.
J: DUDLEY

To Mr Treasurer Taylor
By order of ye Gouerno^r & Council
Is^A ADDINGTON Secr^ty

Vera copia. — *Witchcraft Papers, ut supra,* 64.

F.

(Receipts of claimants for compensation.)

Whereas His Excellency the Governour & Generall Court haue been pleased to grant to ye persons who were Sufferers in ye year 1692 Some considerable alowance towards restitucon with respect to what they Suffered in their Estates at that Sorrowfull time & haue alsoe appointed a Comitte Viz John Appleton Esqr Thomas Noyes Esqr John Burrel Esqr Nehemiah Jewett & Stephen Sewall to distribute ye Same to & Amongst ye parties concern'd as will by ye records & Court orders May appear. Now Know yee that wee the Subscribers herevnto being Either ye proper parties or Such as represent them or haue full power & Authority from them to Receiue thier parts & Shares doe acknowledge to Haue Receiued of & from ye s^d Comitte ye Severall Sums Set against our respective Names in full of our parts & Shares of ye money afores^d & Such of vs as haue orders from some of ye parties concerned to receiue their parts & Shares doe a vouch them to be real & good So that for whomsoeuer wee take vpons vs to Receiue any Such Sum wee doe obleige oursel[ues] to Indemnify y^e Said Comitte to all Intents construcons & purposes wee Say Receiued this 19th Day of February Anno Dom 17$\frac{11}{12}$ & in y^e Tenth year of

Abram How For Mary & Abigail How	4 14 0	
Ephraim Roberdes for James Martha and Sarah How children of John How	4 14 0	

John Ames Ten pounds by ord^r of his mother on file	10 0 0
Ephraim Wiles	14 0 0
Abigail Faulkner	20 0 0
marke of George Georg Jacobs	46 0 0

marke of Abraham A Foster for mother 6 10 0	marke of Anne ⊗ Andrew^{e}s 23 0 0 ⎫
marke Abraham A Foster for Mary Lacey by order 8 10 0	John Foster 08 7 0 ⎬ 79 0 0 Charge 01 13 0 ⎭
Samuel Wardel 36 15 0	John King for himself and Sister Reed
Benia Putnam for Sarah Good 30 0 0	
marke of William W Towne for wife widow of Willard ⎬ 6 12 8	marke Christopher ⌒ Read ⎫ maried Eliz. Hoar ⎬ marke Joana ⌐ Green ⎭
Isaac Estey 2 9 0 forselfe	Joseph Parker 8 0 0
John Estey 2 9 0 for Mary Post	Joseph Parker 8 14 0
William Cleves 11 0 0 for M. Carrier.	Joseph Parker 7 6 0

Received as on ye foregoing side.

                        £   s.   d.

Samuel Nurs for himselfe & John Nurse & John Tarbell ⎫
 Rebeccah Preston William Russell Martha Bowden & ⎬ 21 14 0
 Francis Nurse ⎭

marke
Elizizabeth ⌐ Richards alias Procter

marke
Benjam. ℅ Procter

Ebenezer Bancraft for Martha Procter

William Procter

John Procter

Thorndik Procter

In behalf of my self and Joseph Procter and Abigill Procter and Mary Procter and my sister Elizabeth Very

marke
Sarah Munion * ⌐ alias Procter

marke
Elizabeth + Procter

Charles Burrough for my self and for Jeremiah Burrough and Rebekah

                 £   s.   d.

 Fowle Hanah Fox Elizabeth Thomas 4 2 0 each of us — 20 10 0

John Appleton Rec^d for G^o Burrough ye sume of ffore pounds & two shill^s

23^d marke
     Abigail ⌐ Hoar ⎫
        marke   both ⎬ 20 4
     Rebeccah ∪ Hoar ⎭

Feb. 23   marke of
1711   William X Hobbs   9 15 0

    for his Sister Abigail Hobbs   4 2
            Cha   10

             10 0 0.

---

* This word is doubtful.

Leonard ⅔ (marke) Slue for selfe & sister Rachel — 10 4^d.

Mary ⅔ (marke) Pittman alias Hoar

Rec^d as afores^d
for George Abbot & Hanah his wife daughter of Mary Eastey £ s. d. 2 9 0

March 4 1711 by yr written order forty nine shillings
JOHN FARNAUM

March 5 Rec^d for my selfe forty nine shillings 2 9 0
JACOB ESTI.

March 6 1711 Receiud for my selfe three pounds 4 & 6 (s. d.) for my owne Share

Received for our daughter Margaret Willard   HANAH × (marke) WILLARD

Received Ap^l — — — three pounds four shillings 6^d.
WILLIAM ×| (marke) TOWNE
MARGARET ⋀ (marke) TOWNE wife of y^e S^d Wm Towne

Rec^d for my daughter Mary Burroughs four pounds in full for her Share
MARY × (marke) HALL alias BURROUGHS

Mar. 22.   Receiued for my Selfe Ten poundes
17$\frac{11}{12}$
MARY × (marke of) HALL, alias BURROUGHS

Aprill 5, 1712.   Rec̄d of Stephen Sewall as aforesd 6 9
JONA ∪ (marke) WILLARD.

May 1, 1712   Rec̄d on behalfe of my wife Deborah How two pounds seuen shilling in full
ISAAC HOW

Rec̄d for Benj Nurse fifty four shillings & 6^d.
May 12, 1712
SAMUEL NURS

Rec̄d for my selfe ye subscriber & for my Bro^r in Law Peter Thomas in right of Elizabeth his wife and my Sister Hanah ffox wife of Mr Jabez ffox & Rebecca fowles four pounds ten shillings
GEORGE BURROUGS

Receiued for my Bro^r Jeremiah Burroughs & my selfe Two pounds fiue shillings ℔
CHARLES BURROUGH

NEWBURY — May 22, 1712

Rec͞ed for & in behalfe of my wife Jane True & Mary Stanian daughters of Mary Bradbury & for John Buss & Elizth Buss Children of Elizabeth Buss, ye Sum͞ of nine poundes fifteen shillings ℔ me

HENRY TRUE.

May 22^d 1712 Rec͞ed for my Breth₹en & Sisters being Six of vs in Number Children of Judah Moodey one of ye daughters of ye aforesd Mary Bradbury Dec͞d. thre pounds five shill.

CALEB MOODY.

May 22^d 1712 Rec͞d for my Sister Anne Allen & my selfe Children of Wymond Bradbery Dec͞d three pounds fiue Shillings ℔ me

WYMOND BRADBURY

Rece^d for my Two Brothers William Bradbury & Jacob Bradberey & my Selfe } Three pounds fiue Shillings in full

℔ me THOMAS BRADBURY

July 27, 1712 Rec͞d, on ye acc^o afores^d Eleuen pounds fiue Shillings. for my part Rec͞d in full

SAMUEL X PROCTER
marke

Sepr 3^d 1712 Receiue^d for my Brother Joshua & my selfe 4 18 0 which I ingage to produce his receipe for & send to Sewall

BENJAMIN ESTIE

Sep. 3^d 1712. Reced for my Sister Sarah Giles forty shillings which I promise to send her receipt for

BENJAMIN ESTIE

Nou^r. 28, 1712. Rec^d for Joseph Estie & by his written order Forty nine shillings

JOHN COMMINGS —

Witchcraft Papers, ut supra, 65.

G.

(*Copy of the writ in English v. Corwin, and of the return thereon.*)

ESSEX ss.

William the third by ye Grace of God of England Scotland France and Ireland King defender of the faith &c.

| SEAL. | To ye Sheriffe of our County of Essex or deputy or Constable of Salem Greeting. |

Wee Comand you to attach ye Goods or Estate of Capt George Corwine of Salem Mercht. to ye value of fifteen poundes & for want thereof you are to take ye body of ye said Corwine if he May be found in your precinct & him safely keep so that you have him before Our Justices of Our Inferior Court of Pleas to be holden at Ipswich for Our s^d Countey on ye last Tuesday of March next Ensuing Then & There to Answere to Philip English of Salem Mercht in an action of ye Case for that ye said Corwine did by himselfe or by others Imployed by him take & driue away from or near about ye dwelling house of ye sd English in Salem a Certain Cow with bobb Tail, darke couloured & fiue Swine. viz. a large Sow & four shoats ye sd Englishes without his leaue or lycense sometime in August 1692, and doth yet detain ye Same though demand hath been made for them which is to ye plaintiffs damage seuen pounds money as Shall then and there apeare with damages & haue you then there this writt

Witness Bartholmew Gedney Esqr in Salem, This 26th Day of February 1695-6 & in ye Eigth yeare of Our Reigne

STEPH SEWALL

Cleris —

in per su ent to this war rant i haue for want of the goods seased the bodye of the with in mention ned capten georg Cor wing and deliuered or committed him to natthanniel sharp of salem ye gold kepper* February thies 26, 1695-6 and gaue him a coppye of thies writ.

this is a true re turn   atest

JOHN WOOD WELL
constable
of Salem. — *Files of Inferior C. C. Pleas, Essex Co., Mar. 7,* 1696.

---

* Jail-keeper.

H.

(Record of a court of oyer and terminer 1698.)

Hereunder is given the entire record of the first special court of oyer and terminer under the act against piracy and robbing upon the sea : —

At a Court of Oyer and Terminer holden at Boston January the Eighteenth. 1698. *Annoq R R^s Gulielmi Tertii nunc Angliæ &c Decimo*, pursuant to his Maj^{ties} Commission, following —

WILLIAM THE THIRD by the Grace of God, of England, Scotland, France and Ireland, Defender of the ffaith &c —

To our Trusty and wellbloved Thomas Danforth, Wait Winthrop, Elisha Cooke & Sam^{ll} Sewall Esq^{rs}*

Greeting; Whereas by Law it is provided, That all Treasons, ffelonies, Roberies and Confederacies, committed in or upon the Sea, shall be enquired, tryed, heard, determined and Judged in such Countys & places as shall be Limited by Commission or Commissions to be directed for the same, in like manner & form as if such Offence or Offences had been committed or done in or upon the Land, and after the common course of the Laws, used for Treasons, ffelonies, Roberies, Murthers and Confederacies, done and committed upon the Land. Know yee that, wee have assigned you or any Three of you (whereof either of you the beforenamed Thomas Danforth, and Wait Winthrop wee will to be one) our Justices, for this Time to enquire by the Oaths of Good and Lawfull men Inhabitants of our County of Suffolke within our Province of the Massachusetts Bay in New England, and by other ways, Meanes and Methods by which the Truth of the Matter may be the better known, of all ffelonies, Robberies and confederacies committed in or upon the Sea by one Jacob Smith of Boston, within our County of Suffolke afores^d Marriner. And therefore Wee command you That at Boston afores^d, at a certain day before the Twenty third of January next comeing, which you or three of you (whereof either of you the before named Thomas Danforth & Wait Winthrop Wee will to be one) shall appoint for that purpose, you diligently make Enquiry upon the premisses, and all and Singular the premisses hear and determine, and do and accomplish those things in forme afores^d thereupon, which unto Justice appertaineth to be done, according to Law, and such Order, process, Judgm^t & Execution to be used, had done or Made to and against the beforenamed Jacob Smith so being

---

* The following memorandum appears in the margin of the record : —

January 7th 1698-9 M^r. Elisha Cooke having been last Thursday appointed Clerk of the Court of Oyer & Terminer to be held the 18th Instant had his Oath given him this day in the presence of Elisha Cooke Esqr his Father & Sam^{ll} Sewall Justices of s^d Court —

Indicted and found, as against Traytors, ffelons & Murderers for Treason, ffelony Robbery, Murther or such other offences done upon the Land, as by the Law of Our Province aforesd is accustomed, Saving unto us, Our Amerciaments, and other things to Us thereunto belonging. Also Wee Command you that at the place aforesaid, and day which you or Three of you as aforesd shall appoint, you cause to become before you or three of you as aforesaid Such and so many Good and Lawfull Men of Our County aforesaid by whome the Truth of the Matter may be the better known and Enquired. In Testimony whereof Wee have caused the publick Seal of our Province of the Massachusetts Bay aforesd to be hereunto affixed.

Witness William Stoughton Esqr our Lieuftenant Governour and Commander in Chief in and over our said province, at Boston the Twenty Second day of December in the Tenth Year of our Reign *Annoq, Domini.* 1698.

By Order of his honour the
Lieutenant Governour   W^M STOUGHTON —
with the advice and consent
of the Council.
         Is^A ADDINGTON Secr̄y.
                           Sealed with the province Seal —

By Vertue of the above written Commission, the Justices appoint Wednesday the Eighteenth of January 1698; and accordingly on said Day the Justices did meet, the Commission being read at the opening of the court; The Grand Jury being legaly chosen according to the Tenure of the Commission were Impanneld and Sworne, whose names were these that follow. vizt.

             Nathaniell Williams Foreman —
             John Wing.
             James Hill.
             Joseph Bridgham.
             Bozoone Allen.
             William Welsted.
             John Smith.
             Joshuah Hemmenway.
             John Mayo.
             Jacob Hewings.
             John Capen
             Richard Evines
             Thomas Metcalf
             Sam^{ll} Guild.
             Thomas Swift
             James Brackett.
             Dependance French —

Then Proclomation was made that if any person or persons could Inform the Justices of the s^d Court, the Kings Attourney General, or the Grand Inquest of any Murther, Felony, Roberie or Confederacie done and committed by one Jacob Smith, who stands bound by way of Recognizauce to appear at this Court to answer what should be objected against him the s[d] Jacob Smith on his Majesties Behalf for committing Piracy and Robbing upon the Sea. — No one appearing to declare any thing against the abcve s[d] Jacob Smith, The Attourney-General gave a Bill of Indictment to the Grand Jury against the aboves[d] Jacob Smith, which was as follows.

PROVINCE OF THE MASSACHUSETTS BAY
IN NEW ENGLAND SUFFOLKE ss:

At a Court of Oyer & Terminer holden in Boston in y[e] County of Suffolke in the Province of the Massachusetts Bay in New Eugland, upon Wednesday the Eighteenth of January In the Tenth Year of the Reign of William the Third by the Grace of God, of England, Scotland, France & Ireland, King Defend[r] of the aith &c Annoq Dom: 1698.

The Jurors for our Sover[g] Lord the King upon their Oaths do present
That Jacob Smith of Boston in the County of Suffolke afores[d] Marriner sometime in the year of our Lord one Thousand, Six hundred ninety Six, being in and belonging unto a Barq or Smal Ship whereof one   ffarrer was Master or Commander together with several men more to the number of Thirty or forty (to the Jurors unknown) upon the high Sea, upon or near the coast of East India, or Madigascar, upon the Subjects of the great Mogull, in Amity with our Soverg Lord King William that now is, in the peace of God then and there being, with force and Arms a violent Assault did make, and them in great feare of their Lives did putt, and them wickedly, Mallitiously, felloniously and Piratically did Robb, and from them of their Goods and Chattles, That is to say in money of the Coynes of Several Princes & Nations, Bullion and Gold to the value of two Thousand pounds, of the Currant money of this Province numbred then and there found, did take and carry away Against the peace of our Sov[r] Lord the King his Crowne & dignity, and the Laws & Stattutes in Such Case made and provided

The Grand Jury went out to consider of s[d] Indictment, and Returnd their Verdict thereon Ignoramus, Signed by Nath[l] Williams forem: It is therefore Considered by the Court that the sd Jacob Smith be and hereby is discharged from his Bonds, paying Charges of prosecution. — *Records of Superior Court of Judicature*, 1686–1700, p. 223.

I.

(*List of commissions of oyer and terminer issued during the provincial period.*)

The following is a list of all commissions of oyer and terminer known to have been issued under the provincial government. The date prefixed to each entry is the date of the order in council, and the volume and page referred to are of the executive records of the Council.

May 27, 1692. To enquire of hear and determine for this time, according to the law, & custom of England, and of this their majesties' province, all and all manner of crimes and offences had, made, done or perpetrated within the counties of Suffolk, Essex, Middlesex, and of either of them: — William Stoughton, John Richards, Nathaniel Saltonstall, Wait Winthrop, Bartholomew Gedney, Samuel Sewall, John Hathorne, Jonathan Corwin and Peter Sergeant, commissioners; Stephen Sewall, clerk; and Thomas Newton attorney for the crown (July 26, he was succeeded by Anthony Checkley). — ii. p. 176.

Oct. 22, 1692. To enquire of hear and determine, for this time, all and all manner of felonies, murders, homicides, manslaughters, and other offences, done and perpetrated within the county of York: — Francis Hooke, Charles Frost, Samuel Wheelwright and Thomas Newton, commissioners. — *Ibid.*, p. 196.

Oct. 10, 1696. For the trial of four Indians accused of murder near Hatfield, in the county of Hampshire: — John Pynchon, Samuel Partridge, Aaron Cooke, Joseph Hawley and Joseph Parsons, commissioners. — *Ibid.*, p. 419.

Oct. 14, 1697. For the trial of an Indian at Nantucket, accused of murder: — John Thacher, John Gardner, Matthew Mayhew, Stephen Skiffe and Jonathan Sparrow, commissioners. — *Ibid.*, p. 501.

Dec. 22, 1698. For the trial, at Boston, of Jacob Smith, for piracy and robbing upon the sea: — Thomas Danforth, Wait Winthrop, Elisha Cooke and Samuel Sewall (the justices of the Superior Court) commissioners. — *Ibid.*, p. 569. See provincial stat. 1696, chap. 4.

Nov. 23, 1703. For the trial, at Salem, of Mamoosin, an Indian accused of murder: — John Hathorne, William Browne, Jonathan Corwin, Benjamin Browne, and John Higginson, commissioners. — iii. p. 494.

June 15, 1704. For the trial, at Nantucket, of an Indian, for murder:—John Gardner, James Coffin, Thomas Mayhew, Benjamin Skiffe, and William Gayer, commissioners. — iv. p. 30.

Nov. 8, 1707. For the trial, at Kittery, of Joseph Gunnison for the killing of Grace Wentworth *: — Joseph Hammond, Ichabod Plaisted, John Plaisted, William Pepperrell, John Wheelwright, John Hill, and Lewis Bane, commissioners. — *Ibid.,* p. 479.

Mar. 7, 1711-12. For the trial of Joseph Swaddell, commander of the ship Lake Frigate, of London, for the murder of John Johnston, one of his sailors: — Wait Winthrop, Samuel Sewall, John Hathorne, Jonathan Corwin and Elisha Hutchinson, commissioners. — v. p. 526.

June 5, 1713. For the trial, at Barnstable, of two Indians for capital offences committed in the county of Barnstable: — Nathaniel Thomas, John Otis, James Warren and John Gorham, commissioners. — vi. p. 44.

Dec. 3, 1718. For the trial, at Northampton, of Ovid Ruchbrock, for counterfeiting: — Samuel Partridge, John Pynchon, Joseph Parsons, Samuel Porter and John Stoddard, commissioners. — vi. p. 631. See act of 1718-19, chap. 19.

July 8, 1742. For the trial, at Nantucket, of Harry Jude, an Indian, for murder: — John Cushing, Zaccheus Mayhew, Sylvanus Bourne and Enoch Coffin, commissioners. — x. p. 644. See act 1742-43, chap. 9.

June 23, 1743. For the trial, at Nantucket, of Simeon Howsean [Simon Hew], an Indian, "and any other capital offences": — John Cushing, Sylvanus Bourne, Zaccheus Mayhew, Enoch Coffin and John Otis, commissioners. — xi. p. 54. See act 1743-44, chap. 6.

Aug. 9, 1746. For the trial, at Nantucket, of Jeremy Jude, an Indian, for murder: — John Cushing, Sylvanus Bourne, Zaccheus Mayhew, Enoch Coffin and John Otis, commissioners. — *Ibid.,* p. 652. See act 1746-47, chap. 7.

---

* See The Wentworth Genealogy, vol. i. p. 238.

INDEX

Note:
Page numbers prefixed with an A refer to the first section of the book.
Page numbers prefixed with a B refer to the second section of the book.

ABBOT, George B45
 Hanah B45
ACKERMANN, Nick B13
ADAMS, John B27
ADDINGTON, Isa B43 B49
 Secretary B14
ALBEE, Obadiah B29
ALLEN, Anne B46 Bozoone B49
AMES, John B43
ANDREWES, Anne B44
ANDROS, B4 B26 B37
ANNE, B7 Queen B15
APPLETON, Jno B42 John B10
 B43 B44
BANCRAFT, Ebenezer B44
BANCROFT, B21
BANE, Lewis B52
BARDBERY, Wymond B46
BARKER,
 Ebenezer B39 B41 Jno B41
 John B39 Marya B41
 Mrs B41 William Sr B39
BARKERS, Wm B41
BARNARD, Thomas A14
BARNS, James B10
BELCHER, Gov A20
BISHOP,
 Bridget B12 B17
 Edward B17 B39 B40
BLACKSTONE, A12
BORROUGHS, George B13
BOURNE, Sylvanus B52
BOWDEN, Martha B44
BRACKETT, James B49
BRADBEREY, Jacob B46

BRADBURY, Henry B40 Mary A14
 B40 B41 B42 B46 Sam B40
 Thomas B46 William B46
 Wymond B46
BRIDGHAM, Joseph B49
BROWNE, Benjamin B51 William
 B51
BUCKLEY, Sarah B40
BUCKLY, William B9
BURKE, B31
BURREL, John B43
BURRILL, John B10 B42
BURROUGH, Charles B39 B44
 B45 Go B44 Jeremiah B44
BURROUGHS, B16 Charles A14
 B40 Georg B40 George B11
 B16 B17 B41 B42 Jeremiah B45
 Mary B45
BURROUGS, George B45
BUSS, Eliz B46 Elizabeth B46 John
 B46
CALEF, A9 A10
CAPEN, John B49
CARRIAR, Thomas B40
CARRIED, Martha B40
CARRIER, M B44 Martha B41 B42
 Thomas A14 B39
CHALMERS, B3 B17 B32
CHANDLER, B21
CHECKLEY, B7 B37 Anthony B51
CLEVES, William B44
COFFIN, Enoch B52 James B51
COKE, A11 B24
COLE, Sarah B40
COMMINGS, John B46

COOKE, Aaron B51
   Elisha B48 B51
COR, Wing Georg B47
CORE, Elizabeth B40 Gyles B42
   Martha B42
COREE, Elizabeth B39 Giles B39
COREY, A14 Giles A12 B16 B20
   B42 Goodwife A7 A19 B16
CORWIN, B18 B19 B20 B47
   Jonathan B51 B52
CORWINE, George B47
CORY, Gyles B41 Wife B41
CURRIER, Martha B42
CUSHING, John B52
DANE, A11 Nath B41
   Nathaniel B39
DANFORTH, Thomas B48 B51
DOUGLASS, B31
DUDLEY, A8 B4 B6 B14 B37 J
   B42 B43
DUVAL, B22
EAMES, John B39 Rebecca B37
   B39 Rebeccah B42 Robeccah
   B40
EAMS, Rebecca B41 B42
EASTEY, Mary B42 B45
EASTY, Isaac B9 Isaack B40 Mary
   B40 B41 B42
EMERSON, Joseph B39 Martha
   B39
ENGLISH, B15 B18 B19 B20 B47
   Mr B41 Philip B9 A14 B12 B17
   B47
ESTEI, Jacob B39
ESTEN, Isack B9
ESTEY,
   Isaac B9 A14 B44
   John B44
ESTI, Jacob B45
ESTIE, Benjamin B46
   Joseph B46 Joshua B46
ESTY, Joseph B9
EVINES, Richard B49
FALKNER, Abigail B41
FARNAUM, John B45

FAULKNER, Abigail A5 A8 A10
   B12 B39 B40 B42 B43 Francis
   B9 A13
FFARRER, B50
FFOX, Hanah B45 Jabez B45
FITZHERBERT, B22
FOSTER, Abraham A14 B39 B40
   Abraham A B44 Aen B40 Ann
   B41 B42 Anne B42 John B44
   Michael B24
FOWLE, Rebekah A14 B44
FOWLES, Rebecca B45
FOX, Hanah B44
FRENCH, Dependance B49
FRIE, John B39
FROST, Charles B51
FRY, Jno B41
GARDNER, John B51
GAYER, William B51
GEDNEY, Bartholomew B47 B51
   Mary B15
GILES, Sarah B46
GOOD, Sarah B40 B41 B42 B44
   William B40
GOODELL, A C Jr A3
GORHAM, John B52
GREEN, B B8 Bartholomew A4
   A16 Joana B44
GUILD, Samll B49
GUNNISON, Joseph B52
HALE, B25 Matthew B23
HALL, B16 Mary B45
HAMMOND, Joseph B52
HATHORNE, John B51 B52
HAWK, B18 B24 B25
HAWKINS, B22
HAWKS, Sarah B41
HAWLEY, Joseph B51
HEMMENWAY, Joshuah B49
HENRY, VIII B25 B27
HEW, Simon B52
HEWINGS, Jacob B49
HIGGINSON, John B51
HILDRETH, B21
HILL, James B49 John B52

HOAR, Abigail B44 Dorcas B41
   B42 Eliz B44 Mary B45
   Rebeccah B44
HOARE, Doarcas B39
HOBBS, Abigail B41 B42 B44
   William A14 B44
HOBS, Anigail B40 William B40
HOLBROOK, Abiah B17
HOOKE, Francis B51
HOW, Abigail B40 B43 Abram B43
   Deborah B45 Elizabeth B40 B41
   B42 Isaac B45 James B43 John
   B43 Martha B43 Mary B40 B43
   Sarah B43
HOWSEAN, Simeon B52
HUTCHINSON, A9 B3 B4 A10
   B17 B20 B21 B31 B32 B38
   Elisha B52 Gov A17
INDIAN, Harry Jude B52 Jeremy
   Jude B52 Mamoosin B51
   Simeon Howsean B52 Simon
   Hew B52
JACOB, George B39 B41 B42 Mr
   B39
JACOBS, Georg B40 George B9
   B40 B42 George Georg B43
JAMES, B37 B38 King B5
JEWET, Mr A19
JEWETT, A19 Neh B41 Nehema
   B42 Nehemiah A19 B10 B40
   B43
JOHNSON, Elizabeth A14 B17 B39
   B40 B41 Elizabeth Jr B12 B14
   B17 Francis B17 B39 B41 John
   B9 B39 B40 Mr B39 Mrs B39
   B41 Rebecca B39 B40 Sarah
   B41
JOHNSTON, John B52
JUDE, Harry B52 Jeremy B52
KING, Annies B39 Drcas B40 John
   B44 Mrs B39
LACEY, Mary B42
LACY, Lawrence B39 B40 Mary
   B40 B41 B44
LAMB, B25

LAMBARD, B38
LAMBERT, Nathaniel A16
LASY, Lawrenc B41 Mary B41
LEDITE, Benjamin B29
LENOIR, B22
LISLE, Alice A5
LORING, Israel A20 Parson A20
MANSFIELD, Lord B23
MARSTON, Jno B41 John B39 Mrs
   B41
MARTIN, Susanna B12
MATHER, A9 B9
MATHERS, B9
MAYHEW, Matthew B51 Thomas
   B51 Zaccheus B52
MAYO, John B49
METCALF, Thomas B49
MOGULL, Great B50
MOLTON, Jno B40 Martha B40
MOODEY, Judah B46
MOODY, Caleb B46
MOORE, Dr A3 A4 A5 A6 A7 A8
   A9 A10 A12 A13 A16 A17 A18
   A19 A20 George H A3 B3 Mr
   B4 B5 B6 B8 B12 B13 B14 B16
   B17 B18 B20
MOULTON, John B39 Mrs B39
MUNION, Sarah B44
NEAL, B31
NEWMAN, Thomas B17
NEWTON, B6 B7 B37 Thomas B51
NICKERSON, Ansel B27
NOTTINGHAM, B7
NOYES, Thomas B10 B42 B43
NURS, Beniamin B9 Francis B9
   Georg B9 Iohn B9 Samuel B9
   B39 B44 B45
NURSE, Benj B45 Francis B44 John
   B9 B44 Rebecca A13 B40 B41
   B42 Rebeccah B42 Samuell B40
OLDMIXON, B17 B31
OSGOOD, Capt B40 Mary B39 B40
   Samuel B39
OTIS, John B52
OVERING, Attorney General B32

PALFREY, B21
PARKER, Alice B12 Jno B40 John
  B9 A14 B39 Joseph B9 A14
  B39 B40 B44 Mary B39 B40
  B41 B42
PARSONS, Joseph B51 B52
PARTRIDGE, Samuel B51 B52
PEASE, Mrs B39 Rob B41 Robert
  B39
PEPPERRELL, William B52
PHIPS, B7 B17 B29 B32 Gov A9
  B33
PINSENT, B19
PITTMAN, Mary B45
PLAISTED, Ichabod B52 John B52
PORTER, Samuel B52
POST, Mary B39 B40 B41 B42 B44
POWNALL, B32
PRESTON, John B9 Rebeccah B44
  Samuel B39 Sarah B39
PROCTER, Abigill B44 Beniamin
  B9 B39 Benjam B44 Elizabeth
  B12 B40 B44 Jno B40 John B9
  B39 B40 B41 B42 B44 Joseph
  B44 Martha B44 Mary B44 Mrs
  B12 B42 Samuel B46 Sarah B44
  Thorndick B40 Thorndik B9
  B39 B44 William B44
PROCTOR, John B42 Mrs B42
PRYNNE, B24
PUDEATOR, Ann B12
PUTNAM, Benia B44
PYNCHON, John B51 B52
QUINCY, B21
READ, Christopher B44 Wilmot
  B12
REED, B44
RICH, B15 B16 Thomas A19 B16
RICHARDS, Elizabeth B44 John
  B51
RITCHIE, B22
ROBERDES, Ephraim B43
ROBINSON, B19
RUCHBROCK, Ovid B52
RUSELL, William B9

RUSSELL, Lord A5 William B44
SAINSBURY, Mr A5 B13
SALTONSTALL, Nathaniel B51
SCOTT, Margaret B12
SERGEANT, Peter B51
SEWALL, B6 A19 B33 B46 Maj
  A19 B12 Mr B40 Samll B48
  Samuel B51 B52 Steph B47
  Stephen A16 B11 B14 B15 B38
  B40 B43 B45 B51
SHARP, Natthanniel B47
SHIRLEY, B17
SIDNEY, Algernon A5
SKIFFE, Benjamin B51 Stephen
  B51
SLUE, Leonard B45 Rachel B45
SMITH, Jacob B23 B48 B50 B51
  John B49
SPARROW, Jonathan B51
STANIAN, Mary B46
STODDARD, John B52
STOUGHTON, B6 B7 B9 B33
  William B49 B51 Wm B49
SWADDELL, Joseph B52
SWIFT, Thomas B49
TARBELL, John B9 A14 B44
THACHER, John B51
THOMAS, Elias B17 Elizabeth B17
  B44 B45 Isaiah B17 Nathaniel
  B52 Peter B17 B45
TOWN, Willem B39
TOWNE, Majeret B40 Margaret
  B45 William B45 William W
  B44
TRUE, Henry B40 B46 Jane B46
  Samuel B40
TUCKER, Ichabod A16
UPHAM, B21 Mr B12 B19
VERY, Elizabeth B44
WARDEL, Samuel B41 B44
WARDELL, Samuel B42 Samuell
  B40 Sarah B40 B42
WARDWELL, Mrs B12 B42
  Samuel A14 B12 B14 B37 B39
  B42 Sarah B12

WARREN, James B52
WASHBURN, B21
WELL, John Wood B47
WELSTED, William B49
WENTWORTH, Grace B52
WHEELWRIGHT,
   John B52
   Samuel B51
WHORE, Drcas B40
WIGGIN, J K A16
WILD,
   Ephraim B40
   Sarah B40 B41 B42
WILDE, Sarah B42
WILDES, Ephraim A14
WILES, Ephraim B43

WILLARD, Hanah B45 Jno B40
   John B41 B42 Jona B45
   Margaret B45 Mrs B44
WILLDES, Ephraim B39
WILLIAM, B7 III King B47 B48
   B50 King B4 B50
WILLIAMS, Nathaniell B49 Nathl
   B50
WILSON, Joseph B39 B41
WING, John B49
WINTHROP, Wait B48 B51 B52
WITREDG, Mary B40
WOODELL, Mercy B41
WOODWARD, A19 B14 B15 B16
   B34 B37
WRIGHT, Jno B41 John B39

www.ingramcontent.com/pod-product-compliance
Lightning Source LLC
LaVergne TN
LVHW051707080426
835511LV00017B/2778